THINK
DO
SAY

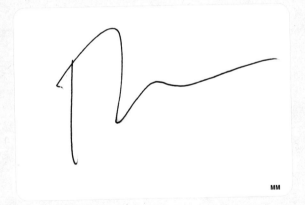

MM

Ron Tite

THINK

THINK

DO

How to seize attention and
build trust in a busy, busy world

SAY

PAGE TWO
BOOKS

Cataloguing in publication information is
available from Library and Archives Canada.

ISBN 978-1-989025-71-0 (hardcover)
ISBN 978-1-989603-10-9 (ebook)

Page Two
www.pagetwo.com

Cover design by Peter Cocking
Interior design by Taysia Louie
Printed and bound in Canada by Friesens
Distributed in Canada by Raincoast Books
Distributed in the US and internationally by
Publishers Group West, a division of Ingram

19 20 21 22 23   5 4 3 2 1

thinkdosay.com

This is for Christy & Max

Contents

• • •

Foreword

. . .

EVEN THOUGH WE'RE around the same age, I want to be Ron Tite when I grow up. And, after reading this book, I bet you will, too.

At a recent strength-based leadership development program, I was asked to choose a leader who has the most influence in my daily life. Immediately, I thought of Ron Tite, even though I don't interact with him on a daily basis. I was then asked to write down three attributes that best describe his contributions to my life. Those, too, came to me quickly:

1   Generosity
2   Egoless guidance
3   Visionary thinking

Ron's work is always in service of other people. Whether he's leading the advertising initiatives for Fortune 50 companies or taking time out to let one of my clients "pick his brain," Ron is there, helping us become not just better at what we do, but better at *who we are*.

Now he's sharing his visionary thinking with you in *Think. Do. Say.*, a book that offers you a unique and effective model for both personal and organizational branding and messaging.

He's the perfect person to deliver this message, because he understands the world of advertising and marketing in a way that few do. Ron is a performer, writer, producer, creative director, and agency owner. He's also a teacher who inspires us while making us laugh out loud.

At my company, Heroic Public Speaking, we see thousands of authors and speakers each year, and we work with most of the A-list speakers in the business. Everyone is unique, but I've never met anyone as generous, egoless, and visionary as Ron Tite. He'll help you think better, do better, and say it better. And he does it without ever mentioning Apple.

Simply put, Ron is best in class—and so is this book.

MICHAEL PORT
Co-founder, CEO
Heroic Public Speaking Worldwide
May 28, 2019

"A book introduction is like an analogue device on a 5G data network. Kinda useless."

• • •

WINSTON CHURCHILL

This Isn't an Introduction

. . .

MOST BOOKS HAVE an introduction.
I don't know why, but most publishers gasp at the idea of not having one.

Apparently, people want a preamble. A rationale. A setup. Or do they?

I respect your time and I appreciate the level of impatience you probably have.

So here's my introduction: Thanks for buying this book. I hope you like it.

Now, let's get to the goods.

"I'm not an inventor. I'm a Thought Leader

and Disruption Evangelist with a focus

on Change Management and Authentic

Engagement. Too douchey?"

ALEXANDER GRAHAM BELL

THE OPT-FOR-CHANGE PART

In a sea of promos and prices, purpose is what people can see from shore.

A Life Lived

. . .

Retail's dead.
Retail's back!
Retail's dead again.
Retail's back!
Who the heck wants to invest in brick & mortar?
Online businesses are investing in brick & mortar!
Sears just went bankrupt.
Amazon just bought Whole Foods!

Depending on the day of the week, retail is either the best or the worst business to be in. Margins are tight, rents are high, and let's admit it, customers can be jerks. But people *do* love a great experience, they want to occasionally see and touch stuff before they buy it, and a street presence can help with brand awareness and distribution.

One thing is certain: Retail is reinventing itself, and not every single shingle will survive. A lot of retailers are in a street fight to stay profitable until they know what works and what doesn't. That's what made the following statement from one retailer's head of merchandising even more jaw-dropping:

| We could never do it, but what if we *close* on Black Friday?

5

Wait, what?

You're contemplating closing your stores on the busiest retail day of the year? You want to shut down when your competition is slashing prices, driving promos, and spending a large part of their budget kick-starting the holiday spending spree? Are you insane?

That retailer is REI and I don't think they're insane. I think they're brilliant.

REI (Recreational Equipment, Inc.) is an outdoor clothing, gear, and footwear company organized as the largest consumer co-operative in the US. Its 6 million active members buy tents, kayaks, mountain bikes, and other outdoor stuff from over 150 retail locations in thirty-six US states and through catalogue and e-commerce channels. It also has REI Adventures, a global leader in active adventure travel, and REI Outdoor School, which teaches courses on outdoor activities.

Every year on Black Friday, REI closes its stores, processes no online payments, and pays its 12,000+ employees to "opt outside" with friends and family. While retail staff at other stores are facing life-threatening injuries from deal-hungry crowds stampeding through the doors like the bulls of Pamplona, REI staff are enjoying the tranquility of taking in a hike or a paddle. Since they began #OptOutside in 2015, 15 million people and more than 700 organizations have joined the movement.

Unlike most "movements," it wasn't created as a response to a creative brief. It was just an idea someone tossed out during a brainstorming session.

It's genius. Here's why: At its heart, #OptOutside is not about a campaign, it's about an action that reinforces a belief. When beliefs and actions come together, great stories are easy to write and worthy of being told.

Here's the full script for the #OptOutside launch spot:

Open on the top of a mountain. A man sits at a desk.

JERRY: I'm Jerry Stritzke, the CEO of REI. This Black Friday, we're closing all 143 of our stores and we're paying our employees to get outside. We believe a life lived outside is a life worth living. We'd rather be in the mountains than in the aisles. Join us on November 27th on opting outside. Thanks.

(Couple hike up to where Jerry is)

MAN: Whoa. Hi.

JERRY: Hi.

MAN: What are you doing here?

JERRY: I work here.

Logo + Super: #OptOutside 11.27.15

There were three pillars behind the incredible growth REI created:

They believed in something beyond their merchandise.
REI couldn't have been much clearer about what they believed. Stritzke said, "We believe a life lived outside is a life worth living. We'd rather be in the mountains than in the aisles." In a sea of promos and prices, purpose is what people can see from shore.

They consciously took actions to reinforce that belief.
Stritzke prefaced their beliefs with a clear indication of how they would live them. "I'm Jerry Stritzke, the CEO of REI. This Black Friday, we're closing all 143 of our stores and we're paying our employees to get outside." He actually mentioned the action before the belief, which gave it a greater priority. To help build trust, REI didn't pay an actor to deliver the message. Stritzke did it himself.

They said it in a simple and memorable way. What an easy story to tell and a simple structure to follow, huh?

1   They stated their beliefs.
2   They described the actions they would take to live them.
3   They described how customers could get involved.
4   They delivered it with an authentic REI personality.

Best of all, they accomplished all this in thirty seconds.

That may be the most efficient and compelling organizational story ever told.

It's a clearly articulated Brand Belief that shows REI cares about more than the products it sells. It supports REI staff and acts as a phenomenal recruiting tool. It announces a bold action that flies in the face of convention without trying to look and act rebellious. It showcases a personality who believes that the warmth of a smile resonates better than the knee-slapping of a laugh. It invites consumers to participate through a hashtag but doesn't desperately beg for user-generated content. Finally, it brands the initiative—#OptOutside—not as an event but as an action.

REI did all of this in under seventy words.

Don't worry, I know *exactly* what you're thinking. Did it work?

As an experienced marketer, everything about this feels right. It checks all the boxes in an interesting way, and given the fictional approach to metrics these days, I could find data that builds a case for its success. So, yeah, I could mention that they got 2.7 billion PR impressions in the first twenty hours. Yes, *billion*: 6.7 billion media impressions overall, 1.2 billion social impressions ... blah, blah, blah.

But to me, this is what matters. In the year #OptOutside launched:

1 REI inspired 1.4 million people to spend the day outside.
2 REI posted its largest-ever membership growth.
3 REI increased revenue by 9.3 percent to $2.4 billion.

Think about that.

REI shut down on its busiest day of the year and actually grew revenue in the process.

They got consumers to look. They established trust in the brand. The result was incredible momentum and growth, all because everyone from the CEO to the cashier were aligned on what they thought, what they did, and what they said.

But why did they have to do it in the first place? Couldn't they have just run a Q4 BOGO (Buy One Get One) banner campaign that was announced internally through an impersonal email from the CEO? Couldn't they have just funneled their money into AI like everyone else? Couldn't they have just gotten the team together for a brainstorming session where they spent four days rewriting their mission statement?

Sure. They could have done all of that.

But consistent growth and momentum for people and organizations require a bit more. On one hand, we need to step away from the MBA textbooks and jargon-filled exercises to land in a truthful and honest place that is as compelling as it is simple. On the other hand, we also need to step away from the latest and greatest technologies and platforms to set up for continued success regardless of when the device we're holding is obsolete and when version 2.0 of our sales software is replaced by version 3.0.

Great organizations know it. So do great people.
It's time to be calm in the chaos.
Because the chaos certainly isn't going away.

"I don't know shit. But I do know

not to trust anyone who calls

themselves a 'Growth Hacker.'"

MARIE CURIE

THIS
IS THE
CHAOS
PART

Buying the space is easy. Standing out is not.

Get into a New York State of Mind

• • •

Two ad campaigns I created have been featured in Times Square. As a Canadian ad guy mostly doing stuff north of the border, I was proud when my work made it to New York's biggest stage. I mean, hell . . . if you can make it there, you can make it anywhere, right?

Times Square is the most expensive promotional real estate in North America, with more lights, signs, bells, flashes, and distractions than your average stretch of pavement. The Times Square Alliance reports that signage in the area generates 1.5 million impressions from over 380,000 pedestrians and 115,000 drivers and passengers every day. It may surprise you to find out that over 60,000 people live in the greater Times Square area, too. That's a ton of eyeballs, and they all need something to look at. Brands buy billboards because they want those eyes to look at their ads.

But here's the real problem:

Buying the space is easy. Standing out is not.

When a consumer stands in the middle of Times Square, they don't even know where to look. Every inch of peripheral vision is filled with something that pulls the eyes away. Blinking. Moving. Waving. Animating. Shining. Flashing. Ringing. "Look here." "No, here." "No, here."

Down on street level, it's even worse.
Evangelical preachers are trying to get you to convert.
Buskers are performing for change.
Food carts are hawking street meat.
Scammers are asking for bus money.
Young comedians are papering a local comedy club.

Curbside entrepreneurs are selling everything from T-shirts and theater tickets to recreational drugs and prostitution.

So not only do they not know where to look, they don't know who to trust, either.

They don't know where to look. They don't know who to trust.

Well, I hate to break it to you, Billy Joel, but you're not the only one in a New York state of mind, because today, Times Square isn't just isolated between West 42nd and West 47th. It's everywhere.

Times Square is in Kentucky.
It's in Winnipeg.
It's at your desk.
It's in the middle of your living room.
Times Square is in your pocket.

It doesn't matter where they're located. Consumers, prospects, clients, and colleagues don't know where to look and they don't know who to trust.

Consumers Don't Know

Consumers are standing in the middle of Times Square bombarded by non-stop promotions across 500 different media platforms, consumed with content at home, at work, and in the car. The unification of church and state (content and advertising) means they don't know what's news, what's advertising, or the difference between the two. They're constantly being sold something by someone, whether it's a fashion influencer they follow on Instagram or a high school acquaintance in need of sponsors for a bike ride to cure cancer.

Consumers don't know where to look and they don't know who to trust.

Clients Don't Know

Clients are in the middle of Times Square. In my world, I certainly feel for our marketer clients. Their brand agency wants to be their social agency. Their social agency wants to be their brand agency. Their PR agency wants to be their ad agency. Their strategy consultants want to be their digital agency. Their media agency wants to be their programmatic trading desk. Their broadcast company wants to be their production company. And Facebook and Google want to be everybody. Everyone wants to solve their problems and everyone wants the budget to do it.

Your clients don't know where to look and they don't know who to trust.

Your Team Doesn't Know

When deciding who to listen to, who to learn from, and what strategy to implement for a successful career, your people are in the middle of Times Square. They see big established companies going down without notice, they're constantly looking for the best-before date on their skill set, they're trying to figure out who their boss is in the dotted-line matrix reporting structure, and they're reading all the books, listening to all the podcasts, following all the thought leaders, and taking all the courses—not to grow their career but to save it.

Your team doesn't know where to look and they don't know who to trust.

You Don't Know

When it comes to your own career, you're standing in the middle of Times Square, too. You're told that artificial intelligence is the answer to everything . . . except relationships, sales, HR, leadership, management, finance, and marketing. Every ten minutes your boss pops his head above your cubicle wall to ask what your strategy is on the thing he heard his nephew talking about. Your spouse wants you to slow down. Your colleague wants you to speed up. And your friend wants you to quit so you can both create that start-up you've always discussed. Everyone's talking about their "why" and all you have is a "huh?" You were told to embrace failure, and now that you're failing, no one wants to embrace you.

You don't know where to look and you don't know who to trust.

Your Personal Life Doesn't Know

Maybe the answer to life, the universe, and everything is out there (forty-two!) but it's buried in the middle of a blog post and nobody can focus long enough to scroll down to see it.

Times Square is in your pocket. It's poking you. It's bugging you. It's distracting you. It's an email arriving.

It's a notification that you've just been tagged in an Instagram post. It's an app telling you the chance of rain. It's the score of the ball game. It's an entire music library that you don't even own. It's a video from that big thing that happened last night. It's a meme starring Kanye. It's countless beautiful photos of your child that you can access anytime. Even if your phone does actually ring, it's usually just, "Hi, it's Sharon, your Google Specialist."

Even when you're at home, you don't know where to look and you don't know who to trust.

Times Square Is Your Time

• • •

The challenges and opportunities of Times Square are in front of all of us. Simply being there isn't enough. You think that you and your message are critical, but to the person on the receiving end, you're just another blinking sign saying, "Look over here. Look over here."

Just because you paid for the eyeballs, that doesn't mean they'll look.

Just because you say it, that doesn't mean they'll hear it.

Just because you write it, that doesn't mean they'll read it.

Just because you've managed your career, that doesn't mean you'll succeed.

Most organizations want to grow. So do most people. But the path to growth, success, happiness, engagement, raises—and bliss, ponies, and butterflies—doesn't look like it used to.

Great brands, great companies, and great leaders are based on what they think, what they do, and what they say. When all three of those pillars work together, people look up.

Getting them to do that has never been more difficult.

"Getting people's attention is almost

as difficult as having a civil political

discussion on Facebook. WTF?"

CONFUCIUS

THEY DON'T KNOW WHERE TO LOOK

It's not just the ads. It's the explosion of products *behind* the ads that's the real problem.

Get Them to Look at You

• • •

In between watching the latest episode of *Queer Eye* and pushing out an Instagram Story of their yoga class, people need to eventually buy stuff. They need to know where hamburger meat is on sale or which shelves to buy for their new distribution center. They have to look up from their passions and seek out their answers.

But when they do come up for air, they have no idea where to look.

Let's take banking.

There used to be, like, five banks. They paid the same interest on the same three types of accounts and they were in your neighborhood. There was the blue one, the green one, and the red one, but it didn't really matter because you didn't choose a bank. You inherited your bank from your parents. It was part of your DNA along with your smile and your aversion to country music.

Now there are more banking products from more financial institutions delivered in more ways, each with their own promotional arm. Grocery stores are banks. Cable companies are banks. Retailers are banks.

Credit unions aren't banks but they're starting banks. Airlines have credit cards. Car companies have credit cards. There are savings accounts, high-interest savings accounts, checking accounts, money market accounts, transactional accounts, private banking accounts, and more. There are ETFs and GICs and RESPs and credit lines, and that's just skimming the surface. On top of all that, there's branch banking, mobile banking, phone banking, internet banking, and robo-banking. When it comes to paying, you can pay directly from your bank or with a check, a debit card, a credit card, a money transfer, an e-transfer, a digital wallet from your phone, a digital wallet from your search engine, or PayPal.

Easy peasy, right? Apparently not.

It's not just banking, either. It's every category from telco to tacos. People don't know where to look because of the growth in the number of products before them. While organizations have been bowing down at the altar of innovation, the reality is that many innovate by cranking out new SKUs of existing products. One has less salt, one has more salt, and one has those characters from the movie *Frozen* on it.

Each has its own ad.
Each has its own content.
Each has its own sponsorship.
Each has its own YouTube channel and Twitter account.

Many talk about the huge growth of advertising (stay tuned for more), often citing the tired, "The average consumer sees 5,000 advertising messages a day." But it's not just the ads. It's the explosion of products *behind* the ads that's the real problem.

There's more stuff. In more places. With more people selling it.

That has led to more pitch slapping than ever before.

Cue the Pitch Slap

• • •

The term "pitch slapped" is such a brilliant expression, isn't it? Some people think I created it, but for the record, I didn't. I heard it in a meeting from Jordan Pollacco of Impact XM. He heard it from a guy who heard it from a woman who heard it from someone else. If I knew who came up with it, I'd give credit. Now I just assume it's an expression in the ether, like, "You can lead a horse to water..." (Which should finish with "but he'll probably ask for a tequila when he gets there.")

Lower costs of production and instantaneous global distribution are great for photographers, musicians, and documentary filmmakers, but they're also great for brands, thought leaders, and scam artists, who can produce more promotional material and put it in more places at a fraction of the cost. And boy, have they.

Cue the Pitch Slap.

Mailing a million people used to come with significant cost, time, and effort. Emailing a million people happens with a click, and it's available to anyone from the biggest enterprises on the planet to a Girl Guide looking to sell cookies through Mailchimp.

Cue the Pitch Slap.

Let's face it, people are exhausted from getting pitch slapped. Everyone has a pitch. Everyone has a promo. Everyone's selling something. People are producing epic amounts of content, lining feeds and walls with promotional messages. The average person doesn't know where to look, but they're also afraid to look because of the pitch slaps they know they're going to get once they lift their head.

Consumers Are Pitch Slapped

Consumers used to have to put up with print ads, TV ads, radio ads, and the odd billboard. Now? Ugh. (Big breath in.) Washroom ads, highway ads, grass ads, gas pump handle ads, gas pump monitor ads, gas pump poster ads, mobile ads, banner ads, programmatic ads, Facebook ads,

By the time you read this, a media agency will be selling branded tattoos on the cracks of plumbers' butts because "it's never been done before and there's plenty of real estate available."

Instagram ads, pre-roll ads, native ads, search ads, retargeting ads, direct mail ads, influencer ads, product placement ads, radio ads, TV ads, podcast ads, and ad ads. If there's an open space, a free pixel, or a silent moment that doesn't have an ad dollar attached to it, just wait. They're not just in your face, either. It's like they're in your soul. You check out a pair of boots on a website and for the next ninety days those boots will follow you around the internet for an Omnipresent Pitch Slap (OPS, naturally).

More ads create more clutter, resulting in a decrease in ad performance, so marketers invent new ads which create more clutter resulting in a decrease in ad performance so marketers invent new ads which create more clutter... This isn't the Circle of Life *The Lion King* promised! By the time you read this, a media agency will be selling branded tattoos on the cracks of plumbers' butts because "it's never been done before and there's plenty of real estate available."

Cue the Pitch Slap.

Your Colleagues Are Pitch Slapped

The average consumer has it pretty bad, but the office isn't the safe haven it once was, either. In addition to emails and phone calls from vendors, partners, and

suppliers, your colleagues are inundated with mentorship programs, social committees, and internal volunteer
initiatives. Every third email is someone asking to "pick
their brain." They get all-staff reminders to clean out the
fridge, and they're sent libraries of information along
with the urgent direction, "FYI." Sadly, "Management by
Wandering Around" has been replaced by "Management
by Reply-All."

Cue the Pitch Slap.

Your B2B Clients Are Pitch Slapped

A couple of years ago, my agency, Church+State, was
approached by a global consulting firm looking for acqui-
sitions. It wasn't something we really entertained, but
what was interesting was when their lead partner said,
"We don't need your roster of clients. We need to increase
the services we provide for our current clients."

They don't want more clients. They want more *from*
their clients.

They're not alone.

No partners are happy with their cut of the client's pie.
They want more. They may not be asking for it directly,
but between basketball tickets, insincere promotion
congratulations, behind-the-scenes C-suite meetings, and
subtle digs like "we can help you with that," every client is

They don't want more clients. They want more *from* their clients.

exhausted from the implied pitch slaps meant to slightly undermine the other partners around the table.

Cue the Pitch Slap.

You Are Pitch Slapped

You'd love to connect with that old friend to just balance out the karma in your life, but you can't because you have 6,554 active Facebook invites, including an engagement party, a gender reveal party, a bachelor party, a book club, a mothers' group, and a candle party. You're expected to support your friends' book launches, improv shows, GoFundMe campaigns, charity runs, kids' school calendars, and affiliate marketing links. You get asked for recommendations for dinner in Chicago, beaches in Indonesia, and what new shows are great on Netflix. Google has a billion-dollar search algorithm, but your forgotten friend from high school would rather activate "the hive mind" for instructions on how to cook kale.

Cue the Pitch Slap.

I'm Pitch Slapped

With my fingers in a number of business units, I'm pitch slapped repeatedly from a variety of different angles. I have the scars to prove it. Usually I'm open to genuine networking requests where an exchange of perspective is valuable to both of us. Still, I get pitches from production companies and directors looking to shoot our stuff, creatives looking for creative mentorship, clients and former clients looking for career advice, students looking for direction on how to start, entrepreneurs looking for heavily discounted creative work, and people who want to know how to write or publish books, and most of all, at least 600 times a day, I get someone who wants to know how they can be paid to speak.

I'm not complaining. I'll often say to others, "Let me know how I can help," and I mean it. I try to make time for as many coffees and phone calls as possible. It's professional courtesy, and I need to repay the countless others who made themselves available to me. It's not that it shouldn't happen. It's that we all need to be more aware that it does.

I'm pitch slapped. You're pitch slapped. Your clients are pitch slapped. Your colleagues are pitch slapped. And the average consumer is pitch slapped.

So not only do they not know where to look, they're pitched slapped so often, they don't know who to trust when they're asked to look.

THE FLIP CHART

Like many of you, I love LinkedIn. The content is great, the network is helpful, and the community challenges my thinking. It also frustrates the hell out of me because so many people use it as pitch-slap central.

Here are the most notorious LinkedIn pitch slappers:

1. THE GROPER

Forget about polite conversation and getting to know you. The Groper initiates inappropriate contact right out of the gate. When LinkedIn asks, "Would you like to add a personalized note to the invitation?" the Groper responds with, "Yes. In the actual invitation, I'd like to immediately talk about what my lead-generation company does, describe how we can help the target's business, and ask whether they're available for a call the next day between 12 and 2."

Response: Don't touch it.

2. THE STUMBLE UPON

After appropriately connecting, the Stumble Upon just casually mentions that after wading through the jungles of social media, they stumbled upon your profile before weakly illustrating that you're the perfect person to pitch slap. How one stumbles upon profiles when you have to initiate viewing a profile is beyond me. I'd also prefer to connect with people who are more targeted in their browsing. Go home, Stumble Upon. You're drunk. (Or you're supposed to be on Imgur.)

Response: Click. Archive.

3. THE SMOKE BLOWER

Wow. Who knew that your incredible experience, wonderful content, unique perspective, and celebrated success would be that obvious through a few job titles, an undergrad degree in sociology, and a couple of recommendations from friends who owe you favors? The Smoke Blower notices and is sure to mention how awesome it must be to breathe the same air as you in a post-connection message before launching into a Grade A Pitch Slap complete with a PDF attachment labeled "Our Capabilities."

Response: You'll cough up hickory.

4. THE HOWDY PARTNER

The HP doesn't know you. They've never met you. They don't live near you. They don't even work in an industry closely related to yours. No bother. You two should discuss a partnership where you can help each other out. They can send business your way and you can send business their way because that's what partners do, partner.

Response: Part ways.

5. THE MOTHER—OR FATHER—TERESA

Some people are just so willing to give. Especially complete strangers who fall over themselves trying to help you solve whatever ails you or gets in the way of complete and total happiness. "So, Ron," they ask. "What can I do to help you?" after initial pleasantries are out of the way. Part of me desperately wants to say, "Do you know any hit men? I need something taken care of."

Response: I'm fine for now, thanks.

6. THE SCRIPT FOLLOWER

You know when you get a call from a telemarketer and you can hear their eyeballs moving as they read the pre-approved script that sounded fine when it was written but doesn't even come close to matching how people actually talk in real life? Well, the Script Follower does that, but in written form on LinkedIn.

Response: I'm sorry. All of our agents are currently helping other customers. Your message is very important to us and will be answered in the order it was received.

7. ROBBIE RANDOM

Hey, connection. What's your favorite bagel?

Response: The one with the hole in it.

My good friend Mitch Joel wrote a brilliant piece called "Not Everyone Is a Prospect," in which he articulates the problem with these types of pitch slappers (only he calls them "Spammers"):

Spammers don't just waste our time, they steal our attention . . . and if all you have is time . . . then all you have is attention. Your time and attention is not a renewable resource, but spammers don't care. They need as many people as possible seeing their message, because the small percentage of those who fall for it . . . makes it worth it to just spray that message and pray. What if these people realized the reality is that not everyone is their prospect?

Now, whenever and however I get pitch slapped on LinkedIn, I just send people the link to Mitch's article.

"I don't care what school you went to. I don't care what jobs you've had. I don't care what your references say. But if you have those tiny little rocket ship emojis beside your name on LinkedIn, I'm not hiring you."

JOHN D. ROCKEFELLER

THEY DON'T KNOW WHO TO TRUST

Being an influencer is not a side hustle, it *is* the hustle.

The Largest Breach of Trust in Consumer Marketing in Decades

• • •

My agency works with large clients like Walmart, Microsoft, Manulife, and others across a wide variety of industries. We help them navigate the unified worlds of content and advertising by creating and distributing relevant messaging to those who will be best served by the brand's products or services. We certainly support the changes made to social platform algorithms, but because of the priority of user-generated content, organic distribution for brands isn't as effective as it needs to be. Brands need to seek out other methods of delivery through partnerships and cash. Sometimes, that includes influencers.

In his book *The Tipping Point*, Malcolm Gladwell detailed how Hush Puppies grew in popularity thanks to a small group of "Connectors." Ever since, brands and consumers have agreed on the importance of those who are cooler, more connected, more informed, and more experienced than the average joe. With so many products and experiences available, people need gatekeepers to point them in the right direction.

We only recently started calling them "Influencers," but we've always had influencers. Elvis Presley was asked to influence behavior in 1956 by getting vaccinated against polio before an appearance on the *Ed Sullivan Show* in hopes of closing the immunization gap with teens. The thinking was, if Elvis got immunized, maybe teens would get immunized. They did. Well, that's all right.

Sonny and Cher were asked to help get people to read the bible. Doris Day was paid to get people to buy International Harvester steamrollers. And the Flintstones were paid to get people to smoke Winstons. Yabba-Dabba-What?

The biggest difference between today's influencers and yesterday's celebrities-who-influenced is that most of the current guns for hire only have social media bullets. Generally, they're not well-known actors or best-selling musicians or authors. They're only famous for being internet famous. They're Instagram Zsa Zsa Gabors. Being an influencer is not a side hustle, it *is* the hustle.

At the beginning of their rise, influencers were micro media companies with loyal audiences built through compelling content creation, true social engagement, and authentic voices. They created stuff brands couldn't, had opinions brands didn't, and delivered it in a tone that brands never would or could have. At a time when traditional media companies were selling their soul, influencers were just naturally expressing themselves without the conflict of an inherent sales bias. Refreshing, right?

My wife and I experienced the benefit of this natural expression. When we traveled to Berlin, we didn't consult any tourism websites or *Lonely Planet*. We built our entire itinerary based on the honest and indirect suggestions from a Canadian expat living (and sharing) her life in Berlin on Instagram. The cafés and restaurants we visited were based on her real experiences and reviews. The best part was that she didn't even know it. She didn't charge for it, either.

At my agency, the first influencer I worked with was Marc Smith of Marc My Travels. (Full disclosure: Marc has since become a friend but wasn't when we started working with him.) On behalf of our client, Patak's, we asked Marc to explore ethnic cooking. For thirty days, he visited ethnic restaurants, prepared ethnic meals, and hosted ethnic-themed dinner parties. Even though Patak's brand presence was really subtle, Marc drove three times as many recipe downloads from the Patak's website as a $100,000 cross-platform investment with a food-themed broadcaster. He also did it for a fraction of the cost. This is just one example of many. In the beginning, influencers were surely worth the investment.

Some still are. Others represent the largest breach of trust in consumer marketing in decades.

Consumers followed and listened to influencers because they didn't pitch slap. They authentically and responsibly discussed the products they used, and they did it without compensation so they could be trusted. But brands needed real voices, dove into the world of "pay to play," and started sending free samples and offering full compensation for product reviews.

Once fees were introduced, some influencers not only sold their souls, they sold out their audiences. Their once-authentic voices became parrots for brands, repeating—verbatim—what brands told them to say. You remember Scott Disick's Instagram post for Bootea Shake, right? He posted a pic of himself with the product and wrote the following caption to accompany it:

> Here you go, at 4pm est, write the below.
>
> Caption: Keeping up with the summer workout routine with my morning @booteauk protein shake!

His post was a copy/paste of the actual instructions he was given by the brand or their agency. He wasn't alone. Naomi Campbell did it. Ramona Singer of *Real Housewives of New York City* did it. Instagrammers

In the beginning, influencers were surely worth the investment. Some still are. Others represent the largest breach of trust in consumer marketing in decades.

@LittleMix did it. It wasn't just that credible voices were being bought, it was that the influencers cared more about the money than the message. Consumers lost faith and trust, meaning every positive brand post was now accompanied with the thought, "Did they *really* like that new curling iron or were they just being paid to say so?"

On top of that, some influencers became entitled, asking to barter positive reviews for free accommodation or a free meal. After YouTuber Elle Darby asked for a five-night free stay at the White Moose Café in Dublin in exchange for featuring it on her social channels, she wasn't only refused, she was called out. Embarrassed, she had to respond with a video apologizing and explaining her actions. What shouldn't be lost in the exchange is what Paul Stenson, the owner of the White Moose Café, said about the controversy: "It puts into question the authenticity of influencer marketing," because "She would have spoken nicely about the hotel only because she was getting it for free."

Not so great for consumers. And even worse for marketers.

Buying traditional media has independent checks and balances in place to ensure viewership and readership numbers are legit. Not so in social. With brands charging by the size of the audience, some influencers inflated their numbers by simply buying followers or subscribing to the incestuous follow-back scheme where the entire industry colludes to inflate each other's communities with the unwritten rule of "you follow me, I'll follow you." They employed bots, faked audience sizes, manipulated engagement, and bit the hand that retweeted them.

They sold out. They cashed in their audience's trust for free products and direct compensation. They lied about their audience size. They inflated fees. They didn't provide any real credible data about their effect. It's even come full circle, with some influencers acting as if they're selling out even though they haven't. A late 2018 trend was posting content to look as if it was sponsored, even though it wasn't. Oh, brother.

Marketers have lost trust.

Consumers have lost trust.

Before long, it seemed like marketers and consumers simultaneously shouted what Elinor Cohen wrote in a piece on Medium in January 2018:

> **It's time to address the elephant in the room: Influencers don't really influence anything or anyone!**

Look, we'll always need influencers—however we define them—to show us what we should aspire to, to point to what's cool and what's not, and to be the gate-keepers we desperately need. Our agency still runs some

Once fees were introduced, some influencers not only sold their souls, they sold out their audiences.

influencer programs with a small group of people we trust, whose value we appreciate, and who we confidently compensate.

For a lot of people, though, the shine is off. Influencers destroyed trust.

Sadly, they're not the only ones.

Trust Lost Market Share in Every Category

• • •

Not only is the consumer completely exhausted from not knowing where to look, they're absolutely fried trying to figure out whether the people and brands worthy of winning their time are also worthy of winning their budget. With so many options to choose from, distri-buted through so many new methods of delivery, supporting so many new business models, using so many new technologies—how can anyone know who to trust anymore?

They can't. And they don't.

Let's face it, the consumer's mindset about business is often affected by their mindset outside of business, and when it comes to trust in general, Joe and Jill Public have thrown up their hands in frustration. Lance Armstrong lied to our faces. The Panama Papers accomplished nothing. The 1 percent got richer. "America's Dad," Bill Cosby, turned out to be "America's Predator." The police stopped protecting and started harming. Politicians sent dick pics to anyone with a data plan. Trump lies more than he blinks. Almost half of the men in Hollywood left people yelling, #HimToo?! The Russians stole the election. Cambridge Analytica stole our data. There are fake Amazon reviews. And bots providing service that used to be done by humans. Is it any wonder that the period we're in is often referred to as the "Post-Truth Age"?

People are now so skeptical that they don't turn to members of the clergy for the truth. They turn to *Adam Ruins Everything*. Trust has become a premium product with an incredibly short shelf life.

Consumers Don't Know Who to Trust

Over and over, promises were made to consumers—life would be better or faster or cheaper or leaner or cleaner or greener—but the truth behind the promises hinged on whether consumers were willing to read the six inches of legal birdseed that followed the phrase, "Some conditions apply." What consumers wanted was the truth. Brands responded with, "You can't handle the truth! So here's an asterisk and some legal disclaimers instead."

Beyond the subtle half-dishonesty, some businesses just went and ahead and blatantly destroyed consumer trust. Volkswagen cheated on emissions. Wells Fargo created fake accounts. Papa John said the N-word. Theranos went from $9 billion to nothing overnight. Apple was throttling older iPhones. Uber was being run like a frat house from the '70s. Equifax had a data breach. Huawei may be spying for the Chinese. There's a new headline about Facebook every day, it's usually followed by a Google headline, and no one is entirely sure what Amazon's actually up to.

To consumers, life has just been one big Fyre Festival of trust, making their purchase decision motto, "It's probably too good to be true."

Your Colleagues Don't Know Who to Trust

If consumers have been tainted by broken promises, your colleagues have been left skeptical by broken mission statements. They don't know what works or who wins. Old guard execs bonus themselves while their outdated business models crumble. The new guard nouveau riche cash out after starting and selling businesses that have never shown a profit. In an age of chaos where people fear for their jobs, your colleagues have been left feeling like they've been volun-told to appear on a corporate version of *Survivor*, repeatedly hearing the mantra "Employees are our most valuable asset" just before Jeff Probst finishes that week's episode with, "The Senior Management Tribe has spoken. We wish Carol the best in her future endeavors."

Your colleagues used to laugh at "Dilbert." Now they're living it.

Your Clients Don't Know Who to Trust

When I asked my friend and co-founder of Simmons Sharpe, Bill Sharpe, what the biggest factor contributing to the downfall of the big ad agencies was, he was unequivocal in his response:

> **The erosion of trust. It's gone from gradual to escalating and then to almost structural.**

He's right. Agencies have been shown to have their heads up their denim-covered behinds on so many issues. Inflated fees that lead to the hiring of cost consultants. A lack of accurate performance data. Little desire to really embrace digital. Media agencies owning their trading desks. Paying for banner ads that were never seen by

What consumers wanted was the truth. Brands responded with, "You can't handle the truth! So here's an asterisk and some legal disclaimers instead."

consumers. Fake clicks. Fake sites. Fake people. Bots outnumbering humans. Inconsistent definitions of video views. And a yearly jaunt to sit on yachts and sip champagne in Cannes. No wonder marketers lost trust. Former CEO of Reddit, Ellen Pao, responding to an article titled "How Much of the Internet Is Fake? Turns Out, a Lot of It, Actually," went one step further when she tweeted:

> It's all true: Everything is fake. Also mobile user counts are fake. No one has figured out how to count logged-out mobile users, as I learned at reddit. Every time someone switches cell towers, it looks like another user and inflates company user metrics.

You Don't Know Who to Trust

You're the only one who truly cares about you. Everyone else has a bias. Your boss wants your loyalty. Your subordinates want your job. Your vendors want your budget. Your clients want your time. You've heard promises about your role. Promises about your compensation. Promises about your team. The only direction you've been given is to "innovate," but no one has told you what that actually means, and no one has given you the budget to explore it or the forgiveness to get it wrong. Instead, you spend more time creating the illusion of innovation than truly innovating. You don't know where to turn for true and trusted advice. You keep searching and searching and you've read so many "The 7 Things That Successful People Do Every Day" articles that you want to vomit from the clickbait. (BTW, the one thing that successful people probably *don't* do every day is read articles titled "The 7 Things That Successful People Do Every Day.")

Here's the thing. People used to vote with their wallet. Now they vote with their time.

Often, who they trust is who they listen to.
Who they trust is who they buy.
Who they trust is who they recommend.
Who they trust is who they promote.
Who they trust is who wins their time.

They don't know where to look. They don't know who to trust.

What are you going to do about that?

THE FLIP CHART

Part of the reason there's a lack of trust within business is because of language. It's hard to trust someone who carts out the same hollow expressions that have been used over and over again with disappointing results, like Jack Donaghy before a board meeting. If you want to build trust, make sure these tropes don't pass your lips.

LET'S TAKE THIS OFFLINE

Translation: I have no idea what that means, so instead of appearing weak and indecisive in front of my peers, I'm going to suggest that we discuss this at another time and in another place—preferably never and nowhere.

BHAG

"Big Hairy Audacious Goal" was coined by Jim Collins and Jerry Porras to mean a "long-term goal that changes the very nature of a business's existence." Instead, BHAG has become a manager's testosterone-filled way of making an empty promise to check a buzzword box that is ridiculously unattainable and irrelevant to 99.9 percent of the organization. "Our BHAG is to transform retail!" Really? Mine is to do away with this horrible phrase once and for all. (No offence to Collins and Porras, who had great intentions with their creation.)

THINK OUTSIDE THE BOX

If there's a Bad Business Phrase Hall of Fame, this one got in on the first ballot.

PING ME

I'm sorry. I'm not on Ping. Is that a thing? Oh, it's not a thing. OK. What do you mean? Email? Text? Tweet? Twitter DM? Facebook Messenger? Instagram Message? Smoke signal? What??? There are hundreds of ways of contacting you, and you chose one that doesn't exist.

SYNERGY

I asked my LinkedIn audience (obvi, valid research) and this one was mentioned most. At its core, "synergy" is supposed to define the benefits that will be created when two organizations merge. Then internal buzzword bingo players light-years away from M&A got a hold of it and bastardized it to describe everything from sales and marketing cooperation to the office lottery pool. Used correctly, it's also a fancier way of saying "layoffs." (Don't even think of mentioning "synergizing.")

LEADS

I used to love *Glengarry Glen Ross*. I really enjoyed watching Al Pacino and Jack Lemmon fret about the Glengarry leads while Alec Baldwin gave away steak knives and El Dorados. Now, all I can think about is the email spam, LinkedIn invites, and million lead-generation consultants promising this shallow definition of a prospect I have 0.00006 percent chance of closing. You want leads? Who doesn't?

LEAN IN

Sheryl Sandberg's work is both important and ground-breaking. Finally, someone stepped up and provided realistic guidance and inspiration exclusively to women (and I don't mean to say that in a patronizing tone as a dude). "Lean in" is not just a movement for equality. It will create better leaders and better business regardless of gender. Sadly, it's also being used in boardrooms as a shorthand for focus or attention. I've been in meetings and literally heard people say, "We're going to lean in to Q3." This was supposed to be a term used to inspire gender equality, not the heading for a *Business Insider* article. If you don't use it correctly, can you please lean out?

ASAP

Translation: "I've screwed up. How fast can you save my butt?"

SOLUTION PROVIDER

When your product sucks and the pipeline is dry, that's when senior leadership will gather everyone around for the fateful announcement. You don't sell products anymore. You're a "solution provider." Which means you ask more questions so you can sell more products. Put another way from the *Sloan Management Review:*

> The word solution needs to be retired from the business vocabulary. What was once a meaningful, buyer-defined term that meant "the answer to my specific problem" is now generic jargon that sellers have co-opted to mean "the bundle of products and services I want to sell you."

Finally, I love this comment on LinkedIn from my friend Karen Wright:

> At a PepsiCo International conference years ago I sat next to a British guy who took pages and pages of notes over the course of the days. He finally revealed that he'd been recording all of the "North American business buzz-isms" he heard during the presentations. *His* take on the weirdest/least useful? "How the f-k do you stretch an envelope?? :)"

People
used to vote
with their
wallet. Now
they vote with
their time.

Bing Bong, No One's Home

• • •

I have a background in comedy with twenty years of stand-up under my belt. There is a lot to love about stand-up, but what's most important about the craft is not the jokes. It's the insights behind the jokes.

In *Carlin at Carnegie*, George Carlin said, "Well, that's my job . . . reminding you of things you already know but forgot to laugh at the first time they happened." See, stand-ups don't actually create anything. They simply hold a mirror up to society and illuminate the absurdities that already exist.

I don't think there's a better insight about the consumer mindset than what Sebastian Maniscalco explored in his comedy special, *What's Wrong with People?* Through three minutes of brilliance, Sebastian recollects how families used to react when their doorbell would ring:

> Twenty years ago your doorbell rang, that was a happy moment in your house. It's called company . . . The whole family went to the door . . . Nobody looked to see who it was. You just opened up the door . . . Your mother had a little Entenmann's, maybe some Sara Lee crumble cake just in case company came over. She made an announcement

> when she bought it. She's like, "Listen, nobody touch this
> cake. This is for company only. Those crap muffins, those are
> for you people..." Nobody had a cell phone back then, so
> if your house phone did ring, your father said, "Nobody get
> that phone, we got company..."
>
> Now your doorbell rings?

Then, through great physical comedy, Maniscalco mimics a family turning out the lights, silencing the room, hiding from the people at the door, and moving through the house in an army crawl.

And *that* is the state of the world.

Those of us in sales and marketing killed the most important community interaction of all: people stopping by our homes to say hello. After years of pushy bell-ringers interrupting the dinner hour to sell chocolate bars, vacuums, natural gas protection plans, and duct cleaning, average people just stopped answering. It's not that we didn't trust the people at the door. It's that we stopped giving them an opportunity to even make an impression.

Isn't that the perfect metaphor for what most of us are doing every single day?

If you're selling something, you're ringing the doorbell.

If you're marketing something, you're ringing the doorbell.

If you're trying to convince colleagues, you're ringing the doorbell.

You're ringing the doorbell. And no one's answering the door.

You Are Pre-roll

• • •

Pre-roll advertising is the video ad that pops up before video or broadcast content on YouTube and other places. It's the annoying thing that stands between you and the thing you actually came to see.

When the advertiser has selected the skip option, a button appears in the bottom right, saying something like, "You can skip ad in 5 . . . 4 . . . 3 . . . 2 . . . 1" before "Skip Ad" appears. I *work* in advertising and whenever a skippable pre-roll starts, the only thing my eye is fixated on is the countdown clock as it descends toward the promised land. I'm pretty sure I have professional-level click speed as it changes to "Skip Ad."

The Skip Ad button isn't just in pre-roll. It's in every client, customer, prospect, and colleague interaction you have.

And even then, when you're at the holy grail of business interaction—be it through email, Slack, ads, video, blog posts, or face-to-face—they consider you pre-roll. You're the thing that's getting in the way of what they came to do or see. There's a massive Skip Ad that they're hovering above, wondering how long before they can click to escape your interaction.

5

"Entrepreneurs don't write Vision

Statements. Their virtual assistants do."

POPE SIXTUS IV

THEY DON'T KNOW WHAT TO DO

If you thought
it was difficult
relating a mission
statement to
your specific job,
try applying
it to your life.

Old School. New School. No School.

• • •

OK, so you admit that you and your team have some new challenges given the mindset of consumers, clients, and colleagues. Now someone needs to be the Champion of Change so you channel your inner innovator and lead transformation, create disruption, and blue ocean your way back to the top. You organize an all-hands-on-deck meeting at the Ritz-Carlton in Maui to present a strategy that will increase the "Return on Wow" (ROW). You print posters that say, "ROW Together!" and you bring in Ladysmith Black Mambazo to lead the company in a musical performance of "Row Your Boat" using nothing but their voices and hotel champagne flutes. You return home and cross your fingers that it works.

Sadly, this isn't far off from how some business leaders want to bring about change in an organization. And some of you are no different in managing your own careers.

Around December 30th you start making resolutions about how THIS year is going to be different. You sign up for a gym membership, promise to get to the office early every morning, begin Margaret Atwood's MasterClass, and start a TikTok account because you read that you should. You write "YOLO" on a yellow stickie, paste it to your cubicle wall right next to the faded "Far Side" cartoon of the kid pushing on the school door that says "Pull," and crank out a deck that outlines your BHAG for the coming quarter: "To credentialize my aspirations and add value to value for real value." Then you randomly connect with twelve new people on LinkedIn and curate a post by Richard Branson. Within eight days you're back to complaining about your boss.

Again, I'm obviously exaggerating the scenario, but IMHO, it's not far off.

When faced with seismic change, when they don't know where to look or who to trust, organizations and leaders tend to default to one of two approaches (or both):

1. They Kick It Old School

There's a reason your CMO got her executive MBA at a prestigious business school every third weekend over three years. She's been desperately waiting for a chance to apply her learning. It's as if Henry Mintzberg is in a breakout room screaming, "Release the hounds!" And boy, does she.

Before you can say "move the needle," she'll bring in consultants to recraft the mission, hire a facilitator to reimagine the vision, complete a SWOT analysis leading to the Four Pillars of Success, apply to be certified for the latest iteration of ISO 9000, initiate a full CX review so the company can truly become customer-centric, and, naturally, redesign the logo, write a new tagline, and change your CEO's title to "Chief Excitement Officer."

Here's the problem: It takes the entire organization working together in complete unison to really drive organizational momentum and growth. And 99.9999 percent of the organization didn't go to business school, doesn't care about a SWOT analysis, and has never known the difference between mission and vision, let alone how either of them relate to their specific function. Old-school kickers try to change the organization with the *McKinsey Quarterly*, but most of their people are checking out BuzzFeed.

1(b). You Kick It Old School

Wanting to build momentum in your own career, many of you will employ the exact same tactics as your Harvard-trained leaders. Over coffee with friends and colleagues, you'll refer to it as "Reigniting your Personal Brand." You'll craft a Personal Brand Mantra, redo your Myers–Briggs profile, articulate your own SWOT, write a value statement, and make yourself the CEO of *you*. It's OK to be using the metaphor for personal development, but if you thought it was difficult relating a mission statement to your specific job, try applying it to your life. Don't worry, though, you're on the right path! Keep reading.

2. They Kick It New School

"You know what this organization needs to become a category of one?" your boss asks the emotionless faces crammed into the main boardroom and waiting for the big brilliant reveal. "Snapchat."

Yup, when your organization's ecosystem changes, some think the best strategy is to throw money at contemporary tactics even though the C-suite has a rudimentary understanding of the new platforms (at best). So you're directed to start purchasing hardware and software for a Big Data push to the cloud, organize Hack-a-Thons to unearth a culture of disruption, start

Here's the problem: It takes the entire organization working together in complete unison to really drive organizational momentum and growth. And 99.9999 percent of the organization didn't go to business school.

running ads on Instagram, install vending machines that only accept cryptocurrency, create an innovation "lab" so your clients think you're cooler than you are, and go all-in on social, producing content for Facebook, hiring a community manager to handle customer service complaints, and building a nimble war room so you can tweet stuff during the Academy Awards. Also, uh . . . "Something-something blockchain."

Without a strategic foundation, a responsible approach to development, or a full understanding of the people and process implications, these tactics are rarely successful and, worse, are obsolete when 2.0 launches.

2(b). You Kick It New School

You join Facebook to understand the platform. You start following people on Twitter so you can curate great content. You join Instagram to see how food companies are using Stories. You dial up LinkedIn because the B2B content is great. You start a podcast to establish thought leadership. Three weeks later, you're not sleeping because you can't keep everything straight. Besides, you just end up arguing politics on Facebook, retweeting celeb gossip on Twitter, sharing pics of your baby on Instagram, and looking for jobs on LinkedIn, and your podcast is dead after three episodes from apathy.

It's Time for Primary School

. . .

I'm not anti-education and I don't complain about the downtown elitists in management with their big fancy degrees. It's not that it's wrong to go old school and do that work. Hell, I helped launch an executive MBA at a very prestigious business school, so I know the importance of academic models to business success.

Still, true organizational change doesn't end with those biz school exercises, it starts there. Most of the people within an organization have been through enough company-wide transformation initiatives to know that if they just wait long enough, there will be another one soon enough. Remember, they don't know who to trust, so spare them on the lecture on why *this* time it's really going to work.

Your mission statement is irrelevant if your people don't know exactly how they can live up to it. Your vision is irrelevant if they can't see themselves in your future. Your personal brand *is* important, but it should be based on action, not on mantras. Embracing new trends and new technologies is important, but they come after the answer.

That's where we're at. Where do we go?

"They" can be your consumers.

"They" can be your clients.

"They" can be your prospects.

"They" can be your colleagues.

"They" can be your senior management.

"They" can be you.

Whoever "they" are, they've had it.

The number of choices and options before them is dizzying.

They're getting pitch slapped from dawn until dusk.

They're skeptical beyond belief.

They don't even trust the people they know, let alone someone new selling a new thing in a new way.

What are you going to do about it?

Are you going to sit on the porch ringing the doorbell?

Are you going to be happy being treated as a pre-roll ad, converting less than half a percent of the time you show up?

Are you going to talk to yourself, ignore your people, and kick it old school?

Are you going to check some boxes and try to game the system with vanity metrics just to say you've gone new school?

If you're an organization, you need everyone unified. You need to be aligned in action.

If you're a person, you need to align the perception of who you are with who you really are.

You need something that allows for the big brains to connect with big hearts and big hands.

It needs to be deep enough to be strategically sound.

It needs to be flexible enough that it can evolve as the world does.

It needs to be accessible enough that not only can everyone understand it, they're inspired by it.

It has to have a little bit of old school, a little bit of new school, and a little bit of no school.

It needs to be customizable enough for use by the company, each of its departments, all of its people, and you.

Especially you.

You didn't think I'd lead you down this road and not give you what you came for, did you?

"Deliver on your promise. If you advertise that your new room deodorizer smells like watermelon and it actually smells like apricots, I'm going to be pissed."

ARISTOTLE

THINKING AND DOING AND SAYING

Companies don't perform. People do.

TDS

• • •

Great organizations and great leaders get people to pay attention to them, they get people to trust them, and they align the actions of all those around them to generate momentum and growth. They don't do this based on some perfectly written mission statement or some hollow buzz-words, or by chasing the latest tactic.

They do it with these three pillars:

1 What they think
2 What they do
3 What they say

Think: What do you believe?

When everyone is pimping product and promos, it's no wonder people don't know where to look. When people and companies move from being product-focused to being purpose-focused, they elevate the conversation to something people actually care about. REI doesn't believe in selling tents or discounting sleeping bags. They believe that "a life lived outside is a life worth living." This not only helps them cut through, it helps establish a foundation that is independent of products. They've been able to develop revenue streams—like their outdoor school and travel group—that wouldn't fit into tradtional retail product-based beliefs.

Do: What do you do to live your beliefs?

Clients and consumers don't know who to trust because they've experienced decades of companies claiming to believe in something, only to find out through the company's actions that they don't. Believing isn't enough. You have to act to reinforce your beliefs. These actions are based on who you do it for, what they want you to do, and who you do it with. REI supported "We believe a life lived outside is a life worth living" by closing on Black Friday.

Say: How do you spread the word?

If you believe in something greater *and* you behave in a way that reinforces that belief, it's worth talking about. And if you're going to talk about it, you should say it in a way that gets as many people onside as possible. Just state what you believe, say what you do to live it, and say it in an authentic and memorable way. REI had the CEO say it with their unique and honest personality.

Think. Do. Say. It's all three working together. You can't cherry-pick and focus on just one.

If you believe in something greater *and* you behave in a way that reinforces that belief, it's worth talking about.

All Think

As an organization, if all you do is think, think, think, without any doing, you're a think tank. I'm willing to bet there aren't many think tanks reading this book. Even academic institutions do stuff. Thinking is critical, but there's no money in the mind.

As a person, if all you do is think, think, think, without ever doing anything, you're a philosopher. And in a world where every template-designed Maya Angelou quote on Instagram justifies someone having "philosopher" as a job title, philosophizing has become a commodity. Go beyond the brain.

All Do

If your organization just does random stuff without any of it ever being strategically aligned, then you're probably a sweatshop with turnover issues. Sweatshops aren't fun. They leave you exhausted and unsatisfied because you never reach a finish line. Hint: An organization can't reach the finish line if no one agrees on the race they're actually running.

If as a person all you do is do, do, do, without being strategically aligned with the direction of the organization, you may not be as popular as you think you are because you're probably defining your success by the number of hours you work as opposed to the quality of those hours in delivering on the purpose of the organization.

All Say

If your organization just talks about the things that you're going to deliver, but you never actually deliver them, your customer churn is probably through the roof. That means you constantly have to cut your margin through rebates and promotions to acquire new customers. Unlike the all-Doers, the all-Sayers' race is very clear. It's a race to the bottom.

As a person, if all you do is talk about the things you're going to do but never actually do them, you'll be found out.

It's about thinking *and* doing *and* saying. One feeds the other.

Together, they create organizational and personal momentum and growth. REI did it. So can you.

An organization can't reach the finish line if no one agrees on the race they're actually running.

Forward...March!
Drive Organizational Growth

• • •

When you're trying to get people to look at you and trust you, it's critical that you deliver with flawless execution every time at every touch point. That's why people love brands in the first place. Good brands offer up a consistent experience with their products, their people, and their environments. A Big Mac in Pittsburgh tastes the same as a Big Mac in Plano. The Big Mac prepared by Frank is *exactly* the same as the Big Mac prepared by Francesca. Every. Single. Time. The Big Mac is always there. The Big Mac will never let you down.

Full disclosure: I enjoy McDonald's, but I think I'm one of seven people on the planet who has never had a Big Mac. It's obviously not because of health concerns. It's just that the "Special Sauce" freaks me out. Pass the nuggets, please.

While supply chain logistics can be complex, once a worker has the ingredients, it's pretty easy to operationalize the exact duplication of a fast-food item. Employees just follow instructions. "Cook meat patty for thirty-eight seconds. Put this stuff on it. Put it between these buns. Put it in this box." It's not as easy to operationalize more open-ended behaviors like customer service protocol, product knowledge, sales techniques, marketing processes, et cetera. But it's just as important, if not more.

Companies Don't Perform. People Do.

I love delivering this message to customer-facing staff who feel they have no power, no control, and no influence within the organization. The harsh truth is customer-facing staff can have the *most* influence over how an organization performs. Whatever your company is, it's nothing. It's only a legal entity represented by a name and a logo. Truthfully, the company is the sum of all the efforts, actions, and decisions made by all the people within the organization. The performance of the organization is 100 percent on you. It's 100 percent on your colleagues. It's 100 percent on frontline employees, employees in finance, procurement, and HR. Companies don't perform. People do.

The TDS Wheel of Growth

When every person in every department is aligned on what they think, do, and say, and with what the organization thinks, does, and says, you'll achieve total

TDS WHEEL OF ORGANIZATIONAL GROWTH

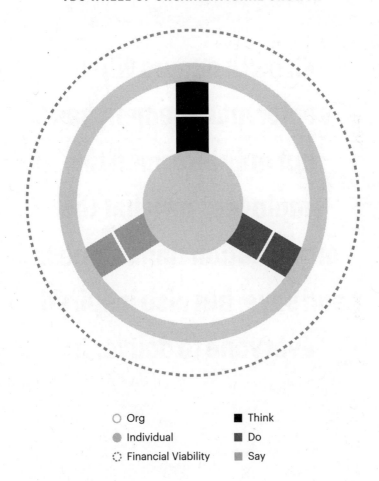

○ Org
● Individual
○ Financial Viability

■ Think
■ Do
■ Say

Growth occurs when senior management has not only informed the employees on what the organization thinks, does, and says, but also inspired everyone to deliver it.

organizational alignment. This total cohesion between purpose, actions, and dialogue is what creates organizational momentum and growth. Growth occurs when your people execute consistent delivery at every possible touch point. That only occurs when senior management has not only informed the employees on what the organization thinks, does, and says, but also inspired everyone to deliver it.

It Only Works if Your Business Model Works

If you're a car manufacturer and you believe it's a human right to destroy the planet, it doesn't matter how well you reinforce that belief and how brilliantly you talk about it, the blatant lack of buyers will destroy your financial viability. If you're an outdoor equipment retailer who believes that people should enjoy the outdoors, and what you do to support that belief is give away your products, your business model won't work, regardless of how aligned your customer-facing staff are.

Point is, the combination of your purpose, actions, and dialogue doesn't guarantee growth, it only delivers it if your strategy is right in the first place. If your business model isn't sound, I'm sorry, but this wheel won't help.

Can I recommend counseling?

March . . . Forward!
Drive Personal Growth

• • •

You might not want to hear this, but regardless of your weight, your buns, or your gross Special Sauce, you're like a Big Mac, too. You have a reputation. It's not about taste— it's about how people feel when they work with you.

When the perception of what you think, do, and say matches the reality of what you *actually* think, do, and say, you get positive personal momentum and growth. Don't forget, while organizations typically have very narrow definitions of growth, you can choose to define it however the heck you want, including happiness, passion, opportunities, money, and more.

TDS WHEEL OF PERSONAL GROWTH

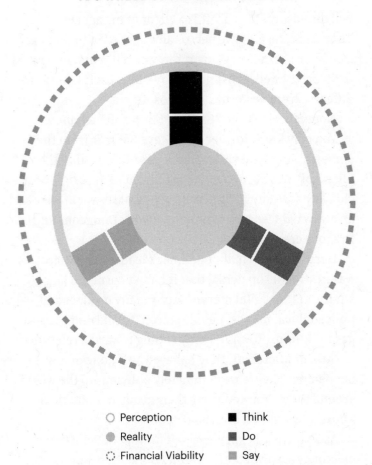

○ Perception   ■ Think

● Reality   ■ Do

◌ Financial Viability ■ Say

Bing It

• • •

Full disclosure: Microsoft is a client of my agency, Church+State, and I've personally worked with them as a creative partner on and off for over ten years. I know them pretty well. Trust me, today's Microsoft is very different from yesterday's Microsoft.

Nope, this isn't the "Ballmer Microsoft" anymore.

You may know former CEO Steve Ballmer from the embarrassing viral video of him parading around the Microsoft World Partner stage in front of 35,000 'softers clumsily screaming, "I LOVE THIS COMPANY!!!" like an awkward teenager trying to rally his Dungeons and Dragons crew.

During the last half of Ballmer's leadership, Microsoft was in straight-up denial that it hadn't cornered large swaths of the digital market. After many product and philosophical misses, people started to murmur that—gasp—Microsoft was quickly sliding toward irrelevance.

Still, *at* Microsoft, they behaved as if none of it was happening. They were completely oblivious to the world around them. You could say their heads were up their Xboxes. I wouldn't, but you could.

As a partner, I experienced it firsthand. Before every meeting, we were subtly reminded that non-Microsoft gear was not to be seen. "You should get a Windows Phone!" I'd quietly think, "Nope." One day, I mentioned that I had "Googled" something and someone piped up with, "Don't you mean you 'Bing-ed' it?" It was embarrassing for all involved.

Enter Satya Nadella.

Nadella took over as Microsoft CEO in 2014, and he had a very different attitude on how to keep Microsoft relevant.

Nadella thought that the inflexibility painted Microsoft as insecure (it did), and that meant that they would constantly be on defense. And defense is no way to innovate.

Soon after being named successor, Nadella gave a public presentation using a non-PC for the onstage demo and Google Chrome as the default browser. During his first public press conference, he announced the first product that would launch under his leadership was Microsoft Office for the iPad. Internally, everyone knew that he described his approach as the "new growth mindset."

Nadella wanted Microsoft products to be things customers don't just need but want, and he wanted to make Microsoft the kind of place that engineers and researchers might choose over rivals. He knew that being able to adapt and integrate with the industry was necessary to achieve that kind of success.

Since his tenure began, Nadella has helped Microsoft's market valuation top $500 billion for the first time since the year 2000. It saw share prices rise more than 30 percent. Microsoft adapted to grow, and Nadella's Think-Do-Say strategy helped get it there.

Think: He believed Microsoft should make stuff that people want to have, not what they need to have.

Do: He oversaw the creation of Microsoft Office for the iPad.

Say: It's a "new growth mindset."

He thought it.
He did it.
He said it.
And he didn't have to use Clippy to remind us.

Fill 'Er Up

. . .

While showcasing Satya Nadella may inspire some of you, it may also turn some of you away. We do that a lot in business. We resurrect Winston Churchill for leadership advice. We turn to a Larry Ellison case study to show us how to be entrepreneurial. And we quote Gandhi when we want our teams to think about values and purpose.

Gandhi? We expect our teams to relate to—and emulate—one of the greatest human beings to have ever walked the earth? I don't know why more people don't stand up and say, "But I'm not Gandhi. I'm just Cathy."

Some people meant to inspire us can actually intimidate us. Let's face it, most of us just aren't Elon Musk or Jeff Bezos. I'm certainly not.

Well, I'd like you to meet Adrian Flinn.

I met Adrian in the summer of 2017 outside of Vancouver. I was touring western Canada for the Co-op, a large regional grocery, gas, agriculture, and farming co-operative. They're an incredible organization filled with some of the nicest and kindest people on the planet. I was helping local Co-ops inspire and inform frontline staff to bring the brand to life through their actions. My presentation wasn't to a group of middle managers like it normally is. It was the people in the trenches: cashiers, deli counter staff, produce people, gas station attendants, and others who had a customer-facing role. These people are the most crucial part of a brand experience, but I almost never get to speak to them. They don't go to retreats in Cuba, and there's no President's Club for someone who says, "Did you find everything you were looking for?" 8,000 times a day. They are a huge part of the DO, but they never gather to discuss how they're actually supposed to do it.

The Co-op's tagline is "You're at home here," and we were discussing what each individual could do to deliver on that brand promise. That's when Adrian spoke up.

Adrian was a student and gas station attendant at Otter Co-op near Abbotsford, BC, southeast of Vancouver. She explained that she found it really difficult to make people feel "at home" at the gas station because she didn't speak the language of a lot of her customers. Abbotsford is home to a very large South Asian community.

So this is what Adrian did: she went out and learned Punjabi.

Yup, Adrian—gas station attendant Adrian, not-even-close-to-the-CEO Adrian—went out and on her own time and on her own dime learned Punjabi. As if that wasn't enough, she also learned American Sign Language just in case she had to communicate with any hearing-impaired customers.

I've met CEOs from the largest companies in the world. I've hung out with Olympians. I know some incredibly talented and successful comedians, musicians, and artists. And I don't think I've ever been more inspired by the actions of any individual than I was when I met Adrian.

Through her actions, Adrian helped the Co-op achieve total organizational alignment, delivered positive momentum and growth for the organization, and created positive momentum for her own career, regardless of whether it's at the Co-op or not. Think-Do-Say? Adrian delivered it all.

She thought that people should feel at home at the Co-op.

She personally behaved in a way that reinforced that belief.

She said it in a way that surprised and delighted her customers. She said it in Punjabi.

When people and companies move from being product-focused to being purpose-focused, they elevate the conversation to something people actually care about.

I'll Have a Grande Racist, Please

• • •

After I resigned from the ad agency Havas and before I started Church+State, I spent a lot of time at Starbucks. I didn't just consume coffee there, I conducted business there. I wrote, held meetings, and took calls. I didn't pay rent, but I'm sure ordering twelve grande lattes a day helped contribute toward the electricity bill.

On April 12, 2018, Rashon Nelson and Donte Robinson did exactly what I had done. They walked into a Philadelphia Starbucks, took a seat, and prepared to have a business meeting.

Moments later, Starbucks manager Holly Hylton didn't just call the authorities, she called 9-1-1. Police arrived and asked Nelson and Robinson to leave. When they refused, they were arrested. Law enforcement took them out in handcuffs.

Nelson and Robinson are African American. You probably know that because another customer caught the whole ordeal on video. If you didn't actually see it, you heard about it. Outrage was immediate (as it should have been). Social media blew up, people were calling for a boycott of Starbucks, and news of the unfortunate incident made headlines around the world. How could this happen? Isn't Starbucks an organization that stands for equality? They are. Wasn't it Starbucks who launched the initiative "Race Together," designed to initiate and inspire a national dialogue on race relations? It was.

Was this act racist? Yes.
Is Starbucks a racist organization? No, I don't think it is.
So, what happened?

It was what happens when organizations and their people are not aligned on what they believe, how they act, and how they talk. I call it an Integrity Gap.

The Integrity Gap

• • •

When people within an organization think, do, and say what the organization thinks, does, and says, total organizational alignment is achieved and the result is Positive Organizational Momentum. It's rainbows and flowers and a massive group hug to celebrate raises for all.

But what about when it doesn't?

What happens when certain individuals *don't* think, do, or say the same things as the organization? What happens when the organization—through the actions and decisions of the senior management—don't live up to the purpose and values promised on the corporate website? What happens is an Integrity Gap.

An Integrity Gap is when people within an organization contradict what the organization supposedly thinks, does, and says. The result is negative brand momentum. And that's never good for business.

The actions of the manager at Starbucks contradicted the values that Starbucks stated it believed in.

"Everyone is welcome": Apparently not.

"Acting with courage . . .": Nope.

"Transparency, dignity, and respect": Not on that day.

The organization states one thing. A customer experiences something entirely different. An Integrity Gap occurs, and in that moment, the brand regresses with negative momentum. So do the people who cause it.

Go ahead and take a look at any huge brand failure. Usually, it's an Integrity Gap.

Remember David Dao being dragged off of United? Julie Elaine's tweet essentially said, "The actions of the staff on this flight contradict what we have been led to believe United Airlines actually thinks, does, and says." She just said it in a far more efficient way: "So much for flying those friendly skies . . ."

Integrity Gap.

Volkswagen lying about fuel emissions? Prior to the scandal, Volkswagen's Values Statement said, "To offer attractive, safe and environmentally sound vehicles which can compete in an increasingly tough market and set world standards in their respective class." Uh, no.

Integrity Gap.

Wells Fargo setting up fake accounts? Integrity Gap.

Dove having a black woman transform into a white woman? Integrity Gap.

Equifax's data breach? Integrity Gap.

And pretty much *every* single social media misstep from brands who almost immediately follow up with "We apologize if we offended anyone." Integrity Gap. Integrity Gap. Integrity Gap.

Sometimes, an Integrity Gap is people-driven. A couple of Domino's Pizza workers shared a video of them putting cheese up their nose and farting on the salami. Those individuals are entirely to blame. Other times, an Integrity Gap is culture-driven. Frontline staff of Wells Fargo opened up a couple of million additional customer accounts without the actual customers ever approving them. It wasn't the actions of a couple of bad apples. It was done by over 5,000 employees. Senior and middle management may not have committed the

An Integrity Gap is when people within an organization contradict what the organization supposedly thinks, does, and says.

fraud, but they did put unachievable quotas in place for new account activations and pressured employees to meet the ridiculous goals. They created culture-driven integrity gaps. If you're going to constantly tell people to "do whatever it takes" to meet their numbers, don't be surprised when they ignore your values.

Integrity gaps can be minor or they can be major. They can lead to one dissatisfied customer who mutters under their breath, or they can lead to one dissatisfied customer whose experience is captured on video, shared around the world, and shown as the lead story on the six o'clock news across the country. They can lead to a negative review on Yelp or they can lead to a massive drop in market cap.

Regardless of what is generated from an Integrity Gap, they should be avoided at all costs.

What Are You Hungry For?

• • •

"Your job is to shut the fuck up."

I actually said that to a colleague once. It may be the worst thing I've ever said in a business environment. To this day, I can't believe those words left my mouth and were aimed at another human being. Especially one I respected as much as I did (and still do).

I'm not proud of it and I would hate to be judged for it. Those who know me know that it's the furthest thing from my character. Those words do *not* represent what I think and how I act. But if the only experience someone had with me was hearing me say that, they'd walk away with a less than flattering perception of who I was. They'd be totally justified thinking that, too.

Because of one negative interaction, the perception wouldn't have matched the normal reality. When the actions of a person contradict what the organization stands for, it's an Integrity Gap. When the actions of a person contradict what that same person actually believes and how they normally behave, it's also an Integrity Gap.

Organizations can have them. People can have them.

Snickers has done a brilliant job of showing how hunger-inspired character shifts can cause us to become completely different people. Summed up with the tagline "You're not you when you're hungry," the well-known Snickers campaign provides a solution to temporary character flaws. When a young man mysteriously transforms into a trash-talking Betty White because he's really hungry, his girlfriend feeds him a Snickers. That brings him back to his normal self.

Snickers is a substantial snack and has been often complemented with the line "Snickers really satisfies," so I know why they chose hunger as the catalyst to the change in behavior. It's interesting that "hunger" is the thing that causes so many of us to abandon our beliefs and act in ways that create Integrity Gaps in our character.

Our hunger for attention.
Our hunger for money.
Our hunger for success.
Our hunger for promotions.
Our hunger for respect.
Our hunger for power.

When a person's hunger for something is stronger than the ethical boundaries that contain them, negative things happen. We break through the beliefs that govern our actions and we do something we regret.

Integrity Gap.

The result can either be a short-term hit to our character or start a downward spiral of behavior where it moves from being an Integrity Gap to a new reality of who we actually are. Doesn't it seem like every day someone famous is standing before a media scrum with their head hung low and mumbling out a scripted apology before they trail off into humiliation? Usually, we're left wondering if the unfortunate choice they're confessing to was an Integrity Gap, or whether we were just stupid to think that they were a better person to begin with.

Not to worry. You'll have Integrity Gaps. Your boss will have Integrity Gaps. Your colleagues will have Integrity Gaps. I've had more than I can count. Do your best to avoid them, but own them when they occur, because what you do immediately following an Integrity Gap will say more about your character than what you did before.

"To think or not to think.

That is the question."

JERRY SHAKESPEARE

(BILL'S COUSIN)

THIS IS THE THINK PART

Your organization should believe in something more important than the bottom line.

Don't Be a Monkey

• • •

October 15, 2004, was a big day for news, a big day for comedy, and a big day for politics. But first, back the truck up.

Under Jon Stewart, *The Daily Show* wasn't just a satire of the news format but a comedic exploration of the political issues themselves. Who can forget its brilliantly branded coverage of the 2000 election, "Indecision 2000"? Through all the elections, the tragedy and aftermath of September 11, an endless feed from both sides of the political spectrum, and media that was becoming as divided as the politics it reported, many saw Stewart as the only adult in the room. He cut through the issues and the personalities involved with an honesty that was as refreshing as it was funny. He may not have been the highest-rated show on television, but in many ways, Jon Stewart was on top of the world.

Still, *The Daily Show* wasn't a news organization. It was a comedy show.

Stewart routinely reminded viewers that he and his team followed a show that featured puppets making crank phone calls. He wasn't there to deliver the news, he was there to *make light of* the news. He wasn't selling news. He was selling jokes *about* the news.

Well, until October 15, 2004.

Then hosted by Tucker Carlson and Paul Begala, CNN's *Crossfire* was a show that, in Begala's words, was "about left versus right, black versus white, paper versus plastic, Red Sox against the Yankees . . ." Normally, they featured two guests from each side of the political spectrum, but on October 15, 2004, they only had one. Jon Stewart.

When a comedian, whose product is jokes, gets a national stage on a network television show, like Stewart had that night on *Crossfire*, they pitch their products. They sit on a couch and perform scripted bits disguised as conversation, they discuss their just-released movies, or they tease material from an upcoming comedy special so you want to see more. They have jokes to sell, and on that platform with that many people watching, it's like they're working on commission. It's sell, sell, sell. Comedians always do it, but it's not what Jon Stewart did in 2004.

Jon was officially on the show to promote his show and his new book, *America (The Book): A Citizen's Guide to Democracy Inaction*. He didn't. Instead, he called out the show for hurting America, for looking to Comedy Central for their cues on integrity, for failing in their responsibility in public discourse, and for being news hacks who were part of "Spin Alley."

Tucker Carlson's response to Jon's initial outburst was what most of us were thinking:

> I thought you were going to be funny . . .

And then he said it.

Stewart drew a line in the sand that no comedian had drawn before.

In one quick exchange, he changed the face of comedy forever.

In just nine words, he solidified an entire genre of entertainment and an important take on the news. In one response, he inspired business leaders and showed how they should act.

Stewart replied, "No. No, I'm not going to be your monkey."

Unlike any comedian before him, on one of the biggest TV stages in the world, Stewart refused to pitch or sell his product. He believed in something that was far more important than his product. Through all his shows, segments, monologues, guests, and political jokes were fundamental beliefs that inspired and informed his humor. On that day, in that moment, Stewart led with the beliefs and left the jokes behind.

Stewart put his purpose before his product. That night may have been comedy's version of Black Friday, and like REI, Stewart closed the store. He didn't go for the short-term win, he played the long game.

And it worked. Because Stewart led with his beliefs, cut through the noise, and established trust. When it came to political discussion and sources of nightly humor, viewers knew where to look and who to trust.

Here's Your Weekend Update

. . .

Saturday Night Live is a comedy institution that has been making us laugh for over forty years, and since the beginning, SNL has featured "Weekend Update" as a central part of the show.

Every Saturday night, SNL sells jokes, just as *The Daily Show* sells jokes. When you laugh, that's a transaction. They sell everything from impersonation jokes and game show jokes to relationship jokes and, yes, news parody jokes. It's great, but let's face it, "Weekend Update" is just another excuse to sell you the same product packaged differently from the rest of the show. It's just a slightly different SKU. It's funny. Really funny. But when we compare the engagement level between SNL's "Weekend Update" and the entire genre of comedy perfected by Jon Stewart, it's not even close. There's Trevor Noah. Samantha Bee. John Oliver. Hasan Minhaj. Stephen Colbert. There are significantly more consumer eyeballs watching more shows and engaged in a significantly deeper way than those that tune in to SNL's "Weekend Update."

They sell the same product: jokes.

They deliver them in the same format: news parody.

But the difference in engagement between "Weekend Update" and Stewart's disciples is huge. It's not because of the talent, the network, or the time slot. It's because Jon Stewart and all those who followed him have a soul to what they do. They believe in something that's far more important than the jokes they tell. People connect with Samantha Bee's values (or vehemently disagree with them) and enjoy the jokes along the way. Viewers applaud Trevor Noah's description that, "you can all be pro-cop and pro-black," which sets them up to laugh when he says, "I guess technically that means you could also be anti-cop and anti-black which would make you, I don't know, Mel Gibson." The serious not only sets up the funny, it's more important.

On the other hand, there are no fundamental beliefs or values at the core of "Weekend Update" to connect to, so we're left to engage on a superficial layer of clever writing and funny characters.

It's not just news parody, either. There's a movement in comedy where many comedians are choosing to put purpose ahead of punchlines.

In the middle of her special, *Nanette*, Hannah Gadsby declares she's not going to use her own personal tragedies, heartache, and sexuality as the source of comedy anymore. The most powerful moments of the show aren't filled with laughter, they are filled with silence. Dave Chappelle's *The Bird Revelation* features the comedian perched on a stool, smoking, discussing all sides of the #MeToo movement with more pauses for reflection than for laugh breaks. In *Make Happy*, Bo Burnham indirectly discusses his anxiety and admits that when it comes to the audience, "Part of me loves you. Part of me hates you. Part of me needs you. Part of me fears you." Mike Birbiglia's *Thank God for Jokes* doesn't end on a traditional big epic mic drop with lasers and fireworks and people leaping to their feet in hilarity. Instead, he ends on a heartwarming plea asking people not to quote him out of context. Heck, even Adam Sandler—one of the most playfully juvenile performers of all time—begins *100% Fresh* with the lyrics, "You got killed by an electric car because you didn't hear it coming," but he ends it with a touching tribute to Chris Farley (I bawled like a baby) and then a beautiful song thanking his wife and his fans with a simple send-off: "Thanks for growing old with me."

They all make their money from jokes. But even comedians know that they make their connections from the soul behind the jokes.

They used to lead with product. Now they lead with purpose.

Which one do you lead with?

Believe in Something Greater

• • •

People may be exhausted from getting pitch slapped, but hey, you have sales targets, and those blankets aren't going to sell themselves, right? I can appreciate your frustration, but it's just not working anymore. You're not going to connect with people pushing product because, let's face it, they're not that interested in your widget. You have no secret sauce, you have no proprietary process, and what you sell is pretty darn close to what everyone else is selling at a very similar price point. No wonder you're not cutting through.

They all make their money from jokes. But even comedians know that they make their connections from the soul behind the jokes.

Don't worry. There's a workaround. Here's what you do: Believe.

Your organization should believe in something more important than the bottom line.

Your firm should believe in something more valuable than the services you provide.

Your brand should believe in something more relevant than the products and features it represents.

You need to believe in something more meaningful than your job title and the tasks you execute.

If the whole world is getting pitch slapped with products, features, price points, and promotions, and almost none of it is unique enough to cut through, is it a surprise that people don't know where to look?

If consumers are bombarded by a barrage of detailed, rational information but aren't getting a sense of the ideals behind those products, is it a surprise that people don't know who to trust?

If you define your career by the tasks you execute and the title on your business card, how will you ever advance beyond the borders you've established for yourself? How will senior management ever get a sense of how you'd behave in another role or situation?

Go beyond the rational. Explore the emotional. Start with purpose. Think. Believe.

What's your Brand Belief?

The Brand Belief

. . .

The Brand Belief is just that. It's a statement that reflects what the brand truly believes beyond its products and services, regardless of whether that brand is a multinational Consumer Packaged Goods (CPG) brand or the personal brand of a middle manager in Boise, Idaho.

At our agency, Church+State, the Brand Belief is the culmination of our entire strategic process, which can include macro-cultural influences, a deep dive on the target, category analysis, brand heritage, and more. Getting clients aligned on a Brand Belief can take half a day meeting with important stakeholders, or it can take six months of client soul-searching, proprietary qualitative and quantitative research, and an international tribunal to reach consensus.

When you arrive at a perfectly appropriate Brand Belief, you'll have a foundation for your products, the thread for all your content, a guide to all the decisions your people make, and something that can mobilize, unite, and inspire all levels of the organization.

Here's all you have to do to come up with your Brand Belief. Just finish this statement:

We believe that . . .

For your personal brand, simply finish this:
I believe that . . .

It looks easy, but it's challenging. Immediately, your management team will probably default to a Brand Belief that features your product. "We believe that Jimmy's Low-Fat Cookies are the best cookies in the world!" Yeah, no. That won't work. That's not a corporate purpose. That's a biased we-drank-our-own-Kool-Aid Pitch Slap of the highest order. If you're doing your personal brand, you may default to, "I believe that sales is more important than marketing" or some other version where you elevate your own role and expertise in the organization's success. Again, no. Dig deeper.

If you think that you can plug a few variables into a spreadsheet, hit Shift+F5, and it'll spit out a Brand Belief, you're wrong. It's an iterative process that can take days or weeks of "How about this?"

One of the most memorable examples is the one we wrote for the Canadian Wildlife Federation. We could have featured the importance of donations or the generosity of volunteers or the beauty of nature. Instead, the Brand Belief we wrote was, "We believe that animals are Canadian citizens, too." Now *that's* a Brand Belief. It's a powerful THINK that easily sets up the DO. It can inspire staff; provide a thread for content, a roadmap for services; help make decisions on where to invest funds; and suggest partnerships.

Here's the important part. We didn't create it in five minutes while reading a book. It was an iterative process that took weeks. Yours should, too.

This Brand Belief Will Give You Wings

Originally from Thailand and repackaged, reformulated, and launched in Austria, Red Bull is now the world's leading energy drink. It's also a wonderful example of a brand that puts purpose before product and has an inspiring Brand Belief. While some of its beverage competitors have led with product features like calories, taste, price, and caffeine, at the heart of the Red Bull brand is a fundamental belief that informs their products, marketing, and culture.

Red Bull's product might give you an energy surge, but the adrenaline rush that you can get from participating in extreme sporting activities is even better. If REI believes that a life lived outside is a life worth living, Red Bull believes that a life lived on the edge is a life worth living. It's that Brand Belief that forms the foundation for every product, every event, every sponsorship, every T-shirt, every team member, and every ad.

If you think that you can plug a few variables into a spreadsheet, hit Shift+F5, and it'll spit out a Brand Belief, you're wrong.

What do they think?

If Red Bull articulated their Brand Belief, it would be, "We believe that pursuing an adrenaline rush pushes you to achieve more and experience more."

What do they do?

Well, in the words of CEO Dietrich Mateschitz, Red Bull "provides skills, abilities, power, etc. to achieve whatever you want to." Beyond that, the company produces content and events that feature heart-pounding extreme sports and stunts, including rally car races, ice cross downhill, skiing in the streets, death-defying mountain biking at Red Bull Rampage, and one-offs like Robbie Maddison jumping the Arc de Triomphe (Vegas version) on a motorcycle. They epitomized their Brand Belief on October 14, 2012, with Red Bull Stratos. To transcend human limits, they worked with experts in aerospace, medicine, engineering, pressure suit development, capsule creation, and balloon fabrication so daredevil Felix Baumgartner could free-fall from the stratosphere. He became the first human to break the speed of sound in free-fall and broke world records for highest free-fall and highest manned balloon flight.

What do they say?

"Red Bull gives you wings."

They think it. They do it. They say it.

Red Bull gets a lot of press (and YouTube views) for the actions it takes, but what's most important is that their THINK not only comes before their DO, it's more important than their DO.

A good friend of mine is Matt Basile. Matt's a chef. You may know him as Fidel Gastro, the star of *Rebel without a Kitchen* and the author of two cookbooks, or from his insanely fun Instagram feed. If you were to take Red Bull's Brand Belief and apply it to cooking, you'd have Matt.

Red Bull approached Matt to see if he would appear in some Red Bull videos. While he loves everything about the Red Bull brand, Matt doesn't react well to caffeine. He politely declined the opportunity, telling them that, unfortunately, he couldn't actually drink Red Bull on camera.

Their response: "We don't care. This is about your attitude, not your beverage."

While most beverage brands would want a spokesperson to stare uncomfortably into the camera, unnaturally holding the product (logo facing out) and smiling before taking a big, refreshing gulp, wiping their

If Red Bull articulated their Brand Belief, it would be, "We believe that pursuing an adrenaline rush pushes you to achieve more and experience more."

mouth and saying something lame like, "That hit the spot!" Red Bull knows that they connect with people who share their values and attitude. Anyone can produce an energy drink. When you connect with consumers on values and fundamental beliefs, enough of those people will buy your product. Some won't and that's totally fine. Take it from the head of monetization for Red Bull Media House North America, Gregory Jacobs:

> If it's authentic [and done well] . . . the audience will know who delivered them the programming. Trust me, you don't have to have the can in hand . . .. When the brand comes first, you turn brand lovers into can buyers.

In 2018, Red Bull converted can buyers 6.7 billion times, up 7.7 percent from 2017. And that's no bull.

Red Bull is now available in 171 countries and has over 12,000 employees. It has a brand value of $10.4 billion, has sold a total of over 75 billion cans, and has made billions for Mateschitz.

Red Bull puts purpose before product and, as a result, moves a heck of a lot of product.

You're on the Right Track, Baby

In my last book (co-written by Scott Kavanagh and Christopher Novais and published by HarperCollins), *Everyone's an Artist (or At Least They Should Be)*, I detailed how business can learn from the artistry of Lady Gaga.

So can you as a business professional.

Large organizations aren't the only ones who can drive growth by starting a Brand Belief that drives all of their decisions. Individuals can, too.

I'm assuming that most of you reading this book are living in countries where—within reason—you could do whatever the heck you wanted. If you're an accountant in a telco, you could be an accountant somewhere else. You quit today and get a job at another company. If you're a real estate agent, you've probably been educated to a level that you could quit selling homes and start doing something else and be somewhat successful and happy. Maybe you'd take a pay cut, but you'd be able to feed your family, survive, and have some success.

So if that's true, why are you working where you're working? Why are you doing what you're doing? What do you fundamentally believe about your role, your job, your career, your pursuit?

Well, it's clear what Lady Gaga thinks. She doesn't put her product first. She doesn't define herself by her role or title. The soul of her work isn't the piano or even music or fashion. It's deeper than that.

Lady Gaga thinks: She believes that people should be free to express themselves.

Lady Gaga does: She creates products and experiences where she freely expresses herself to inform, entertain, and inspire those who need it in order to express themselves. She pushes herself to express herself in the most ridiculous ways (hello, raw beef dress), to push the boundaries of self-expression so others can follow.

Lady Gaga says: "Don't you ever let a soul in the world tell you that you can't be exactly who you are."

Here's what I love most about Lady Gaga. We don't even know what to call her. Is she a singer? A dancer? An artist? A fashion house? An actress? A freak? She has been able to grow her career and DO different things that all reinforce her Brand Belief. She doesn't define herself by her role or the tasks that comprise it, she defines herself by her beliefs.

She thinks it. She does it. She says it.

She's on the right track, baby. Are you?

Believe in Something Even
if It Means Sacrificing Everything

• • •

It's not just Red Bull and Gaga who THINK and lead with purpose. There are countless others that you and your organization can learn from.

The Touchdown

Nike officially believes in "bringing inspiration and innovation to every athlete in the world," but on September 3, 2018, they showed us something critical about Brand Beliefs and corporate purpose. All it took was years of racial inequality, a national anthem, and a professional football player who actually gave a damn.

Of course, I'm talking about Nike's 2018 Just Do It campaign. The full two-minute film featured everyone from LeBron James and Serena Williams to Alicia Woollcott, who was both a homecoming queen and a varsity linebacker, to Isaiah Bird, a ten-year-old wrestler who was born without legs.

A voice-over reads the inspiring script and, at 1:17, says the greatest lesson for leaders, brands, and organizations:

"Believe in something even if it means sacrificing everything."

The voice belonged to Colin Kaepernick, the NFL quarterback who believed in something himself, even though it meant sacrificing everything.

It's easy to have a Brand Belief that conveniently fits your narrative or miraculously aligns with positive business results. But remember what advertising legend Bill Bernbach said: "It's not a principle until it costs you money." Nike had no idea what the business results were going to be after running an ad that featured a controversial activist and a sensitive topic. But they did it anyway. As a brand guy, I think if Nike supposedly stands up for athletes, they're morally obligated to run that ad.

Out of the gate, it appeared as if Nike *had* sacrificed a lot. People lit their shoes on fire, flooded YouTube and Twitter with negative comments, and rallied under #BoycottNike. But in the end, Nike proved something with their unwavering beliefs: consumers want to do business with brands who share their values.

In the quarter they launched the ad, revenue increased 10 percent and North American sales increased 9 percent. In the first week after the ad's launch, online sales increased 31 percent compared to 2017. For his stance, Colin Kaepernick finally reached a confidential settlement with the NFL, though at the time of writing, he had yet to sign with a new team. Both he and Nike chose a purpose. Both stood up for what they believed in. One added billions to its bottom line and one was still unemployed, apparently a victim of collusion.

Believe in something even if it means sacrificing everything.

Nike thinks: We believe that we should inspire every athlete in the world (and if you have a body, you're an athlete).

Nike does: The company makes innovative products, actively stands up for athletes, and motivates the rest of us by sharing stories of athletes who go for it.

Nike says: Just do it.

Corporations used to be seen as greedy, soulless, and driven only by profits, while government was seen as the protector of fairness, human interests, and the welfare of all people. Wouldn't it be amazing if it was business—and more importantly, business leaders—that leads us toward social progress while government and our political leaders try to divide us?

Becoming the Best a Brand Can Get

Faced with losing market share to direct-to-consumer brands like Harry's and Dollar Shave Club, Gillette knew that winning the functional battle was going to be tough. They couldn't just flip the switch on an entirely new business model. They had strong retail relationships and a sales infrastructure that sold through that channel. It wasn't exactly "buck a blade delivered straight to your door," but it's not like people stopped buying blades in retail, either.

For years, Gillette had claimed that its razors were "the best a man can get" with a subtle hint that buying their blades would help users be the best men they could be.

Then something changed.
Harvey Weinstein.
Kevin Spacey.
Louis C.K.
Al Franken.
Charlie Rose.
Matt Lauer.

Two hundred and one powerful men lost their jobs or roles because they were exposed for *not* being the best versions of men. Thanks to Tarana Burke's #MeToo movement, many men stood back and questioned how we were

Believe in something even if it means sacrificing everything.

raised, fathered, coached, and mentored where we would do such horrible things to women.

As a brand that had historically stood up for a traditional definition of manhood, Gillette took a cue from Nike, believed in something, and sacrificed a lot. On January 13, 2019, Gillette declared a new Brand Belief. In my words, their Brand Belief became, "We believe that masculinity needs to be redefined." They communicated that to the world with a controversial spot that questioned whether the current definition of masculinity was really the best a man could get.

Over shots and news footage of subtle and overt sexism, harassment, and bullying, the commercial's voice-over says,

> Is this a best a man can get? Is it? ... We believe in the best in men. To say the right thing. To act the right way.
>
> Some already are. In ways big and small. But some is not enough.
>
> Because the boys watching today will be the men of tomorrow.

Like Nike before them, negative comments flooded social media and the mainstream press. People called for boycotts, were offended by accusations of toxic masculinity, and hated the thought of calling out other men. Luckily, many men supported it, too. Including me. I supported the belief as a guy and as a brand guy.

Here's the danger with it, though: they thought it and said it before they did it. I applaud Gillette on their THINK, but there's a reason that SAY is the last step in this process. Without clear actions on what you are *doing* to live the belief, you open yourself up to ridicule, lack of trust, and accusations of marketing deception for financial gain.

While it's too early (at the time of writing) to get sales data, there are some early indications that the spot worked. Morning Consult's initial data shows that before seeing the ad, 42 percent of respondents said Gillette shared their values. After seeing it, that number jumped to 71 percent. The percentage of consumers who said Gillette is "socially responsible" jumped from 45 to 72 percent. Interestingly, among Dollar Shave and Harry's customers, 56 percent said they were more likely to buy Gillette after seeing the spot.

Gillette thinks: We believe masculinity needs to be redefined.

Gillette does: The company will donate $1 million per year for three years to not-for-profit organizations.

Gillette says: Is this the best a man can get?

We have come a long way since The Body Shop and Ben & Jerry's were the only leading brands with a soul. But we still have a long way to go.

Gillette needs to make very bold decisions and take very active steps to redefine masculinity within its own walls before it discusses it beyond those walls. And by the way, donating profits and cutting a check to a charity is the easiest and laziest DO in the book. That's not the best a brand can do.

People don't know where to look. Make them look at your actions.

People don't know who to trust. Establish it with your actions.

Your move, Gillette.

Be Inspired

I could spend pages and pages discussing brands and organizations that have led with THINK, that believe in something more important and put purpose before product. CVS believed in something more important than profits and stopped selling cigarettes. Patagonia reinforced their belief in the environment by donating the $10 million they got from tax cuts to environmental organizations.

Don't worry, not all Brand Beliefs have to tie big-picture movements to your purpose. Heck, our Brand Belief at Church+State is "We believe that people vote with their time."

IKEA believes everyday life should be better for people.
Tesla believes in renewable energy.
TED believes in spreading great ideas.

Airbnb believes that no matter who you are, where you're from, who you love, or who you worship, you deserve to belong.

Kickstarter believes creative projects often need help being brought to life.

Lyft believes in reinventing the city around people, not cars.

Google believes in organizing the world's data.

We have come a long way since The Body Shop and Ben & Jerry's were the only leading brands with a soul. But we still have a long way to go.

Mission and vision statements are written by people who want to sound smart only to be ridiculed by those who truly are.

Here's What the Brand Belief Isn't

• • •

The Brand Belief can be many things, but here's what it's not.

1. The Brand Belief Is Not a Mission or Vision Statement

I know, I know. Your organization has a wonderful mission statement that is printed on the back of your business card, painted on the wall at reception, and emblazoned on your corporate softball T-shirts. You've committed it to memory and can mouth the words of it as your CEO reads the first slide of every off-site deck. Yeah, there's no better way to inspire a team of diligent professionals than kicking off an all-staff with the words, "Let me just remind you what our mission is . . ."

It's not a vision statement, either (whatever the hell that is). Apparently, there's a difference between mission and vision, but no one can agree on what it is. They're usually written by a team of senior managers with master's degrees in jargon (M.Jg.) who would rather craft something that sounds perfectly corporate than create something people actually understand. Trust me, your frontline employees have no clue what your mission or vision statements mean. They're just words uttered by the great khaki-wearers from head office. Remember all the love I gave Red Bull just a few short pages ago? Yeah, well, this is their vision statement:

> Red Bull GmbH are dedicated to upholding Red Bull standards, while maintaining the leadership position in the energy drinks category when delivering superior customer service in a highly efficient and profitable manner. We create a culture where employees share best practices, dedicated to coaching and developing our organization as an employer of choice.

Make it stop. Please. I've just been assassinated, and the crime was death by jargon.

That's language written by people who want to sound smart only to be ridiculed by those who truly are. Mission and vision statements like this are the result of Group Speak. "We can't forget culture," says the head of HR. "Well, it's also critical that we mention profitability," chimes in the head of finance. By the time custodial services chimes in, the organization doesn't need a vision statement. It needs a vision book.

If you have mission and vision statements for your personal brand, have a look at them. Do they really inspire you with plain and direct language, or did you spend half your time on Thesaurus.com looking for a synonym for "thought leader"? Be honest with yourself. Is anyone inspired by what you wrote?

That's why the Brand Belief is so important. By finishing the statement, "We believe that . . ." every person from top to bottom can understand the soul of the organization and can articulate how they can help bring it to life. Easy to articulate. Easy to understand. Easier to implement.

2. The Brand Belief Is Not a Cause

We all applauded when Audi launched "Daughter," a TV spot during the 2017 Super Bowl that creatively discussed the importance of gender equality in the workforce. This was even before the #MeToo movement had gained worldwide traction. Obviously, it's a critical issue that *every* organization should get behind.

But it's not why Audi makes cars.

It's really easy for a brand to align their corporate purpose with the popular issue of the day, but there are a couple of problems with this approach.

Firstly, it's not corporate purpose, it's corporate philanthropy. Go ahead and fund it and support it, but don't pretend that something that has nothing to do with your product or service can actually be the soul of your organization. Nike wasn't supporting Black Lives Matter or the right to protest at a football game. It supported an athlete. Gillette wasn't *against* toxic masculinity as much as it was *for* redefining the masculinity they had previously used to sell their products.

Secondly, it sets you up for failure. When an organization enthusiastically supports a cause as a corporate purpose, the skeptics fly out and start to apply a microscope to the company's inner operations. Soon after the "Daughter" spot launched, it was revealed that of the fourteen Audi executives, only two were women. It was even worse for State Street, the company who commissioned the *Fearless Girl* statue that stared down the bull on Wall Street. They agreed to a $5 million settlement after a federal audit found that over 300 female executives and fifteen black vice presidents were paid less than peers in 2010 and 2011.

That's not fearless. That's soulless.

3. The Brand Belief Is Not Values

Normally when our agency consults with organizations about their THINK, they immediately go on the defensive. They immediately point us to their website, where they have clearly articulated the four company values conveniently spelling an acronym.

I don't buy it.

I shouldn't read your values. I should experience your values.

I know what organizations do. You get senior management together at a resort, huddle around a flip chart, and start to brainstorm values. Before you know it, you've agreed on four wonderful-sounding words using the first letters to spell something like "RICK" (Risk, Innovation, Creativity, and Knowledge). You update the website, add it to your on-boarding manual, and unfurl posters that say, "Be a RICK," and you think you're good to go.

Nope. First of all, most of the values that organizations select aren't even values. They're buzzwords that you think should be included in your values.

Most importantly, I shouldn't read your values. I should experience your values. And *that's* how you conduct yourself. Usually, values highlight how you behave and how you communicate. Not what you think and what you do.

Remember Enron? They had four values painted on the wall behind their reception:

Integrity. Communication. Respect. Excellence.

How did that work out?

4. The Brand Belief Is Not a Campaign

I've been a part of a few ideas that weren't exactly based in reality. When I was at Havas as a copywriter, one of our Canadian clients was Xerox. The account was brilliantly managed by Liz Falconer before she started Brees Communications. Liz and a team created the "Document Cost Index," which would calculate the costs of a company's total document production and compare it as an index against others in their industry. It would pinpoint where an organization could invest to drive financial and workforce productivity.

In the ads that announced the Document Cost Index, the president of Xerox Canada looked into the camera and said,

> The last thing I want to do is sell you another copier.
> The first thing I want to do is save you money.

I've always loved the simplicity and boldness of that line (H/T: Mary Secord) as well as the strategic thinking behind it (H/T: Simon Billing). The problem was that it wasn't a Brand Belief that permeated the entire organization. It was a campaign generated in the boardroom of our agency. Sure, we created something that put purpose before product, but in reality, selling copiers was the first thing that many salespeople wanted to do. That doesn't mean they didn't want to save their clients money, but they had been trained to put product before purpose. Hell, they had been compensated to put product before purpose. What would you do? In the end, there wasn't much training, there was no company-wide buy-in, and while the campaign was a great one, it wasn't itself a Brand Belief.

Marketing can lead the Brand Belief exercise as long as the outcome is baked in reality, not cooked up by a creative team.

Wheels Down

● ● ●

Your Brand Belief is where it all starts. Creating momentum and growth for you or your organization has to start with what you believe. Wheels can't move forward if there is no pavement beneath them.

Your THINK is your foundation.

It adds the strength and consistency to everything you do.

But do, you must. (That sounds like a Yoda quote.)

Wheels won't go anywhere without a force behind the wheel, either. Momentum isn't generated from the road and it isn't generated from the wheel—it's generated from the friction between the two.

When the actions you take meet the foundation of beliefs, you start to move forward toward growth.

Don't "just do it." Think it. And then do it.

Don't
"just do it."
Think it. And
then do it.

"The only difference between someone

who dreams of being successful and

someone who is actually successful is the

word 'actually.' So suck it up, get off your ass,

and actually do something."

MISTER ROGERS

THIS IS THE DO PART

They THINK,
so they DO.
So should you.

Mi Casa Es Su Casa

· · ·

If I didn't have my wife in my life, my vacations would be very different. I'd just land in a city and improvise my way into dining and accommodation. Luckily, Christy follows influencers on Instagram, reads every public review, downloads city guides, cross-references discount codes, and in the end, we end up staying and eating in the best places for a fraction of the cost. Her philosophy is, "You can never be too thorough." Mine is, "I'm sure this place will be fine."

Remember when we went to Berlin and lived the life of a random person on Instagram? Well, we couldn't sleep where she slept, so my wife did some research on hotels. She was excited by one of her finds, "Casa Camper." When I saw the logo and did a quick perusal of the website, I was too.

Casa Camper is a fifty-four-room hotel in the historic heart of the former East Berlin and the current Berlin's most central borough, Mitte. They also have a similar property in Barcelona. At first glance you'd think Casa Camper Berlin was simply a boutique hotel with a great location and positive reviews, but when I looked, I saw something else. The hotel's logo shared some visual qualities with the logo for Camper, the Spanish shoe brand (once a brand guy, always a brand guy). I dug deeper and learned that the hotel was, in fact, owned by Camper Shoes.

I was curious about the brand extension. I wanted to know the link between shoes and hotels. So I asked. I brought a recorder and I interviewed the general manager on the first day of our stay.

> ME: So. Ummm . . . what's the deal with the hotel?
> HER: What do you mean?
> ME: Why did you open a hotel? You're a shoe company.
> HER: We're not a shoe company.
> ME (perplexed): I know you are. I have several pairs.
> HER: We're a company who *happens* to make shoes, but we don't define ourselves that way.

She went on to explain that the company defined itself by their fundamental belief in the importance of health, simplicity, and design. For years, they had reinforced the belief through the products they made. Those products just happened to be shoes. When they looked at what else they could DO to live up to their THINK, they thought that hospitality was in dire need of an experience grounded in health, simplicity, and design. So they opened two hotels that did just that.

Design: The room wasn't an over-the-top crazy design that made you feel like you were staying in a Picasso painting. It was completely unique (red walls), contemporary (modern fixtures), tasteful (minimalist furniture), and functionally fantastic (everything worked!).

Health: On every floor just above the elevator button was a small sign that said, "Walk down, it's healthier." More impressive was that they invested in stairwells you *wanted* to walk down. Normally, hotel stairwells resemble the opening scene of a *Law & Order* episode, complete with a pool of urine, an empty pizza box, and a dead body. These were painted with bright and bold colors and had art on the walls. The stairwells were just as nice as the rest of the hotel.

Simplicity: You want simple? We got a real breakfast ordered off a menu every morning for free. It wasn't one of those "Continental Breakfasts" that features a month-old danish, a machine that manufacturers pancakes, and miniature Froot Loops boxes, either. It was great. They also had a bar but no bartender. I helped myself to whatever I wanted, wrote it on a slip of paper with my name and room number, and then stuffed it in a box. Done. The drinks were billed to our room. That's simplicity.

As you can imagine, I've stayed in more hotels than any person should, and 99.9 percent of them are completely forgettable. They're all . . . well . . . they're fine. A hotel has to be a special kind of bad or a special kind of good for me to remember it. Casa Camper is one of the good ones. It wasn't because they had a belief that I understood and supported. It was because of what they DID to support the belief. Their belief wasn't revolutionary. Their execution was.

Think: We believe in the importance of health, simplicity, and design.

Do: We make shoes that are simple, healthy, and well designed.

We make hotels that are simple, healthy, and well designed.

Beyond that, Casa Camper did a wide variety of small things at every customer touch point to continually reinforce health, simplicity, and design.

Say: The unique and contemporary design of their communications matched the unique and contemporary design of the hotels. They used simple language and restrained, modern design.

Casa Camper's belief wasn't revolutionary. Their execution was.

One final thing I loved about Casa Camper. They don't sell Camper Shoes there. If you want a pair, hotel staff will direct you to the Camper Shoe store down the street. Better yet, take a bike. It's healthier that way.

Do the DO

• • •

Your THINK establishes the foundation for your actions. It's your guide. Your thread. Without it, you'd be aimlessly executing, madly off in all directions (to reference a great Canadian comedy show). My friend Warren Tomlin, a partner at EY and the former chief innovation officer for IBM (and who many say looks like me), likes to describe these rudderless actions as "random acts of strategy." That's not good.

Once you have the THINK, you really need to focus on the DO.

My friend Scott McKain is one of the best and busiest speakers around. Like the supportive friend he is, he agrees with me. In his great book *Iconic: How Organizations and Leaders Attain, Sustain, and Regain the Ultimate Level of Distinction*, Scott says, "The burgers at Shake Shack are unbelievably good. They are so tasty, I believe that is what differentiates Shake Shack from the standard burger competition. As their customer, I don't give a damn *why* they make them so delicious—I just care that they *do*."

Our actions will be a pretty good indicator of what we believe. I had no idea what CVS thought of health and their role in it until they committed to stop selling cigarettes. I didn't know where PayPal stood on the importance of treating all of their people equally until they pulled out of North Carolina after the state implemented anti-LGBTQ legislation. I didn't realize the San Diego Padres even had any beliefs beyond winning and revenue until I found out that they signed Matt LaChappa—a former pitcher in their system who is confined to a wheelchair—to a minor league contract every year just so that he can maintain his health insurance.

So. Where do you start? How can you guide and prioritize all of your personal actions and the actions of your organization so they reinforce your THINK? Easy. You just answer these questions:

1 What's your Essential Do?
2 Who do you do it for?
3 What do they want you to do?
4 Who do you do it with?

DO → What's Your Essential Do?

• • •

There are a million different actions that an organization can take to bring the Brand Belief to life, but the most important one is the products or services it sells and provides. In your endless possible actions, the "Essential Do" is the most basic *and* the most important.

At some point, all that thinking had better lead to revenue for the organization. Right there, at the heart of your business model, is your Essential Do.

Let's go back and take another look at REI. They believe that a life lived outside is a life worth living, so they provide products for people to buy, adventures for people to experience, and training for people to learn.

The first part is the THINK.

The second part is the Essential Do.

The bridge between them is "SO..."

Your organization believes in something, SO you produce a product that reinforces that.

Red Bull believes that pursuing an adrenaline rush pushes people to achieve more and experience more, SO they produce and sell a caffeinated beverage that energizes people into action. Obviously, Red Bull's Brand Belief wouldn't make as much sense if they made an herbal tea that helped people fall asleep.

Lady Gaga believes that people should be free to express themselves, SO she explores and pushes her expression into uncharted and unconventional directions.

Nike believes in supporting athletes, SO they make products that help athletes (anyone with a body) be their best.

They THINK, so they DO. So should you.

That's step one. You need to do even more to support your beliefs, but with so many different options, how do you even decide what else you should do? Well, that depends on who you're doing it for, what they want you to do, and who you're doing it with.

DO → Who Do You Do It For?

• • •

A couple of summers ago, our agency, Church+State, was doing some content consulting work with the Calgary Stampede, the largest rodeo in the world. We started by doing a deep dive on tourism trends, getting a complete download and brief from the management team on past and expected numbers, and exploring the tension between the cultural heritage of the event and the changing demographics of the Alberta population. There was only one thing left to do: we had to experience the entire spectacle for ourselves.

I'm not exactly a rugged cowboy type, but I had always wanted to go to the Stampede. Luckily, I was able to convince my team that I was the best person to make the trip, gather the intelligence, and report back. I failed to mention that to effectively do my job, I would also have to drink beer, line dance with some Calgary-based friends, and see a concert or two. Don't judge. It's called "commitment to the cause."

As I was roaming through the Stampede grounds, I scanned the horizon for an ice-cold beverage to purchase. That's when I saw them: thirty feet apart, there were two separate lines for two separate places that sold the exact same product in the exact same format. One line had two people in it. The other was so long that a sign at the beginning of the line apologized for the forty-five-minute wait.

Same product.
Same format.
One with a two-minute wait.
One with a forty-five-minute wait.
More on that in a minute (ohhhh, the nerve!).

In Australia in 2011, Coke had become too predictable, and teens and young adults felt like Coke just wasn't talking to them at "eye level."

So Coke did what they do so well. They gathered their marketing team, wrote a killer brief, and asked agencies to pitch ideas to address their challenges. The result was a campaign that helped sell 250 million bottles of Coke to a population of 25 million people.

Impressive, huh?

Since then, the campaign has been implemented in more than seventy countries from Great Britain and Turkey to China, Canada, and the US. Internally, the campaign was known as "Project Connect."

You'll probably know it as "Share a Coke."

This simple concept/complex production initiative customized the iconic Coke bottles and cans with the phrase, "Share a Coke with [insert name]." Lucie Austin was Coca-Cola's director of marketing, South Pacific. As Coke describes it, "The moment Lucie Austin saw her name on a Coke bottle, she knew her team had a hit on its hands." Lucie herself said, "My reaction was childlike. I knew many others would have the same reaction."

She was right. It was a huge hit. In fact, most consumers didn't buy it for other people, they bought it for themselves. There's nothing we like better than the sound of our own name. We're all little snowflakes and connect to things that have been customized for us, our interests, and our lives.

You know how you can be at a packed house party, and even though there are sixty loud conversations happening, you'll hear your name mentioned from the other side of the room? The Coke campaign was like that. In the middle of Times Square, with more beverage options than ever before, Coke made consumers look by calling out their name.

That's why there were two lines at the Calgary Stampede.

Coke had a pop-up where visitors could get a customized Coke bottle with their name on it. They didn't have to worry about searching the back fridges of convenience stores, desperately searching for their one-of-a-kind, half-Hungarian, half-Polish name. They could line up, punch their name into a tablet, and within moments, receive one of the most iconic products in the world with their name on it. They just had to wait forty-five minutes in the line to get it. Thirty feet away, they could buy a Coke with someone else's name on it in two minutes or less.

It was the exact same product. In the exact same format.

People waited forty-five minutes to get one personally branded.

Regardless of what your Essential Do is, remember that you do it for an individual.

You don't do it for a shopper persona.

There's nothing we like better than the sound of our own name. We're all little snowflakes and connect to things that have been customized for us, our interests, and our lives.

You don't do it for a demographic or a psychographic.

You do it for a person. And *that* person will look when their name is called.

Who do you do it for?

The Experience of Customer Experience

Forget downsizing, outsourcing, and change management. The trend that many organizations are exploring, enhancing, improving, and prioritizing is customer experience. In one way, I don't disagree. An amazing customer experience can help win the battle for time, create trust, and build loyalty.

On the other hand, I don't really like labeling it "customer experience." Usually, most people within organizations aren't in customer-facing roles, and when they hear "customer experience," they tune out because they don't feel it's relevant to them. Customer experience? What about Gord in payroll? How does this apply to him?

A great experience for the end customer is important. It's usually delivered by a frontline employee, but if that employee hasn't been paid because Gord from payroll didn't do *his* job, trust me, the customer experience is going to suck.

Yes, everyone inside an organization has a "customer," but no one actually calls them that (or if they do, they get eye rolls). That's why it's easier just to ask, "Who do you do it for?"

1. It's inclusive

Employees shouldn't feel like they have to be customer-facing to be an important part of the team. Gord in payroll may not DO it for the customer, but he does DO it for his colleagues who need to be paid every second week.

2. It's flexible

Obviously, I do what I do for our agency clients, but I also do it for my business partners, the team at the agency, the event managers who book me to speak, and the leaders who me want to inspire and inform their people. I also do it for Speakers' Spotlight, the wonderful speakers bureau I work with who trust that I will deliver to *their* clients. I have a number of different customers. "Who do you do it for?" gives me the flexibility to broaden my obligations without having to put an asterisk beside the word "customer."

Data is
more than
a character
from
Star Trek.

3. It's personal

In addition to doing it for Speakers' Spotlight, I also do it for the people *of* Speakers' Spotlight. On one day, I may do it for Dwight, on another for Elise, and on yet another day, I may do it for Melanie. "Who do you do it for?" allows me to make it personal. Coke may do it for global consumers, but they made it personal by putting the names of the actual people they were doing it for on their product.

Grabbing attention and building trust is *much* easier when we can customize our DO for an individual person.

Operationalizing Personalizing

No one understands who they do it for better than Netflix. It has millions of customers around the world. Each of them has unique viewing habits with different tastes in different genres. I'm no different. I love binging on Netflix. When I do, I enjoy watching crime dramas.

When I go to Netflix, it asks me to select from the two users registered. When I sign in under my user profile, the options before me are shows like *The Killing*, *The Gunman*, and *Another Gruesome Tale of an Unsolved Murder Starring People with British Accents*. When my wife signs in under her user profile, she doesn't see *The Killing*. Her choices include *Downton Abbey*,

Gilmore Girls, and *Whatever the Programming Equivalent of a Hug Is.*

If someone has been killed, Netflix knows that I want to see it. If someone has fallen in love, Netflix knows that my wife wants to see it. Honestly, if the only Netflix available was *her* Netflix, I would have canceled our account long ago.

Netflix isn't just collecting data to broadly get to know who they do it for. They're using the data to customize the delivery of their product to the individual. My Netflix is *my* Netflix. The moment I select my user profile, Netflix isn't doing it for anyone but me.

Data Is More Than a Character from *Star Trek*

Since I'm a creative guy, you might think that I have an aversion to numbers, and in most cases, you'd be right. I completely outsource my financial planning, I didn't even know what cash flow was until five years ago, and the fact that every IP address is just numbers separated by dots scares me.

Still, even I know the power of data. It gives us insights, it tells us what's working and what's not, and more importantly, it allows us to deliver personalized ads, products, content, and support externally. Internally, we can deliver personalized training, compensation, mentoring, and benefits. For years, we all dreamed of a day when we could customize the design of every single experience to match what we needed and wanted at the precise time we wanted or needed it. Hang on to your transporters, Trekkies. That day is here.

Just be careful, because while having the data is easy, applying it isn't.

You can have data that tells you what content individual email subscribers want, but if your team and process aren't built to create twenty-five different types of content to be deployed, what's the point? In just about every new business pitch we're involved with, prospects want to know our proficiency with data, even though they have no operational capabilities to handle it or its implications themselves.

You have to know who you're doing it for. Then you have to build ways for you to connect with that person. McKinsey laid out a very simple operating model that can help you do it.

Data foundation

Collect data so you have a 360-degree view of your customer in real time.

Data decisions

Mine the data to identify indicators along the customer journey. Those indicators will inspire new decisions.

Data design

Once you know who's doing what along the entire customer journey, craft different offers, content, messages, and experiences in efficient ways.

Data distribution

You've created the different messages, now you need a process to deliver and measure them across different platforms. When you do, you not only create a great experience, you generate new insights that get added to the foundation.

Netflix has a data foundation:

They have the technology to collect data on what I watch.

Netflix makes decisions:

They've made a decision to track the shows that I watch to completion and place a higher priority on those genres over the shows that I abandon.

Netflix designs:

They produce and curate content from a variety of genres and design their user interface to have a section with clear recommendations.

Netflix distributes:

They populate the appropriate choices for me into the user interface, in a section that's clearly labeled as "For Ron." The more I watch, the smarter their recommendations get.

Don't worry, this model may seem to be the exclusive domain of multinational organizations with heads of IT, millions in hardware and software, and data warehouses protected like Fort Knox. They're not. Truly knowing who you're doing it for and implementing a process of personalization is not about the tools. It's about the desire to do it. In fact, one of the best customer experiences of my life started with a handwritten note.

Putting Data into Action

I'm not really loyal to any hotel brand, but when I'm in Vancouver, I usually stay at the Westin Grand. I was there once and tweeted out,

> **ME:** BTW... I love the Westin Grand.
> **THEM:** We love you, too! When are you coming to stay with us again?
> **ME:** I'm staying with you now!
> **THEM:** Well, if there's anything we can do to make your day better. Please let us know.

Well, if you're gonna ask . . .

> **ME:** Actually, there was no shampoo in the hotel room this morning.

Many of my female friends look at me in bewilderment when I mention this because they all bring their own shampoo on the road. I don't. I don't need "Ooo Alberto" for my receding hairline and growing bald spot. Whatever's on the counter is what I'm using, and if there's nothing there, I'm happy to use the bar-soap-shaped-like-a-leaf provided at all Westin properties.

While I was out of the room, they replaced the shampoo and apologized.

When I was working in the room later, they delivered a carafe of water, fresh fruit, chocolate, and a handwritten note that said,

> **Dear @rontite, Thanks for being a loyal guest (and follower). We hope you enjoy the rest of your stay and here's a little treat (tweet) from us. Sincerely, The Westin Grand**

Great, huh? Management empowered their people to align their individual actions with the beliefs of the organization, and the result was a wonderful experience and positive organizational momentum. I talked about it all over the world, and occasionally people would send them tweets saying I was talking about it.

When I returned to the hotel a few months later, there was a note waiting for me in my room:

> **Dear Ron, Welcome back. It's a pleasure to have you stay with us again and we're truly grateful for the kind words you say about us during your speaking engagements. To show our appreciation, please enjoy the snacks (we hear they're your favorite) as well as a couple of personal touches in your suite. Stay well, The Westin Grand.**

Having the data is easy. Applying it isn't.

Whoa. Awesome, right? It gets better.

See, I'm a simple man with simple pleasures and rather basic dietary needs, and people who know me know that I can survive exclusively on Diet Coke and BBQ chips. Well, accompanying the note were two Diet Cokes on ice in a champagne bucket and three types of artisanal barbecue chips.

Whoa. Awesome, right? It gets better.

Waiting in the bathroom, beautifully and prominently displayed, were twenty bottles of hotel shampoo.

Whoa. Awesome, right? It gets better.

They downloaded and printed a picture of me with our two dogs outside of our home and put it in a silver frame on the bedside table with a note that said, "Hope this feels like home."

Now compare that to a photocopied letter from the general manager that says "Dear Guest . . ."

This whole exercise isn't about budget or strategy or a new data tool. It's about having the genuine desire to truly connect with another human being.

An organization and its leadership can invest in tools, create new processes, and deliver six weeks of training, but if the individuals within the organization aren't inspired to connect with the person they do it for, all of the time and money is wasted.

When I returned home to my wife, told her the story, and proudly showed her the framed photo, she said, "They're just lucky they didn't put a picture of me in the frame. That would have been really creepy." The next time I was at the hotel, I passed along that feedback to Mitchell Fawcett (now VP of client service at Major Tom), who was responsible for doing it. His response was both hilarious and important: "Actually, we have a policy that we'll only put pictures of people who are staying in the room in the frame . . . because you never know who's bringing who to a hotel room." I desperately wanted to ask about the incident that necessitated the need for that policy.

If you don't see the humor in that, we can't be friends.

If you don't see the importance of it, you're not alone. It took me a bit of time to realize it.

This whole initiative sounds like it's some freaky one-off where one person (Mitchell) was inspired by divine intervention to step outside his daily tasks and be the lone bright light to do something remarkable. We talk about moments like this all the time. It's bread and butter for speakers and authors like me. You've heard many of them—that one person in a massive corporation who does something special that one time, and we put them on a pedestal like they're Mother Teresa. They usually don't work, because without operationalizing the delivery of those one-off moments, they get lost and remain as one-offs. Great experiences are delivered when the one-offs become two-offs, and ten-offs, and more.

Since Mitchell had said they had a policy, it revealed they had done it before. Many times. They probably had a room full of silver frames and a process for finding the right photo, printing it, delivering it to the room with the cards the note was written on, and more.

I don't think I've ever experienced a more customized delivery to me as a person. It was all so simple.

1 They had a process based on what was important (Data Foundation).

2 They took the time and made the effort to find out what I liked through social media and by calling my office (Data Decisions).

3 They printed and framed the photo, wrote the note, gathered the chips and Diet Coke, and grabbed more shampoo (Data Design).

4 They had someone place it all in my room before I got there (Data Distribution).

It blew me away. And drove the right organizational momentum.

When I'm in Vancouver and when it's my choice, I won't stay anywhere else.

You're Not Alone. But You Should Be.

Knowing who they do it for and how to operationalize the customization of products, actions, and communications isn't just isolated to the examples above. I'd recommend you search for even more—especially outside of your industry. If you benchmark your own industry, you'll just copy your competition. If you look elsewhere, you'll be inspired to do something that your competition hasn't thought of. People ignore same old, same old, but look up for something new. Maybe these will help.

Starbucks

I know, I know. They occasionally get it wrong, and there are entire websites dedicated to the hilarious mistakes they've made, but I think Starbucks service significantly improved when they implemented "names on cups." When executed perfectly, it gives the cashier an opportunity to verbally thank customers using their name

("Have a great day, Daniel!"), helps them build deeper relationships with regulars ("Good morning, Robin!"), and makes the customer feel better being served as a person as opposed to a beverage choice. Plus, it makes the whole operation run more efficiently. Before they started using names, baristas would call out, "I have a tall macchiato at the bar!" over and over because the customer didn't hear it. Now, "I have a tall macchiato for Lionel!" cuts through the noise when your name is Lionel.

The most inspiring example is in St. Augustine, Florida, where a Starbucks is situated near the Florida School for the Deaf and Blind, and many of its customers are hearing impaired. In addition to regular service, this Starbucks also has a drive-through. Audio in a drive-through is difficult enough to understand for those with perfect hearing. For the hearing impaired, it's impossible.

Enter Starbucks. They mounted video monitors to complement the audio and they trained all of their staff in ASL so every customer can order visually. Who do they do it for? Well, not just "customers," but hearing-impaired and vision-impaired customers. They aligned their actions with the specific needs of their customers. Love it!

If you benchmark your own industry, you'll just copy your competition. If you look elsewhere, you'll be inspired to do something that your competition hasn't thought of.

Spotify

Like Netflix, Amazon Prime, and other new world media properties, Spotify doesn't just have a pretty good idea of who it does it for: its very product is personalized to the core. Originally, consumers thanked the internet because it created an environment where they didn't need the labels to tell them what to listen to. Cut to a few years and *millions* of songs later and consumers desperately asked, "Can someone just tell me what to listen to?" That's when Spotify stepped in. They said, "We can tell you *exactly* what to listen to." From insightful recommendations and curated playlists that blended reliability with discovery, Spotify is as personal as it gets. You know what I really love, though? The cheekiness of them showing off their capabilities. Over a number of wonderfully similar campaigns, Spotify showed off its chops by sharing some of the data that infused the personalized service. It invited everyone backstage by creatively sharing hilarious insights like, "2018 Goals: Be as loving as the person who put forty-eight Ed Sheeran songs on their 'I love gingers' playlist"; "Dear person who played 'Sorry' forty-two times on Valentine's Day: What did you do?"; and "Dear person who spent twenty-two hours listening to 'Wasted Time' this year: Sounds like time well spent." It's one thing to say that you know exactly who you're doing it for. It's quite another to brilliantly prove it.

Ann Handley

If you don't know Ann Handley, you should. Not only is she the chief content officer for MarketingProfs; an author of some amazing books, including her latest, *Everybody Writes: Your Go-To Guide to Creating Ridiculously Good Content*; and a wonderful speaker who travels the globe delivering entertaining and insightful keynotes; she is also just a kind and loyal friend who connects with people in such an incredible way. She's also one of the funniest people on the planet. Ann asked me to keynote at the conference she runs, MarketingProfs B2B Forum, around the time that my wife and I were expecting our first child. Running a conference is like catching chickens—or herding cats, or fishing mice, or whatever. There are a million tiny details and all of them happen at the last minute. Still, waiting for me when I arrived in Boston was not only a onesie with a bulldog on it (my beloved Rupert—RIP—was a bulldog) and a copy of Jimmy Fallon's kid book, *Your Baby's First Word Will Be Dada*, but also a handwritten note inside a card that said, "You're the shit" on the cover. Most thank-you gifts are a mug with the company's logo on it. Ann not only took the time to customize the gifts; the tone of the gifts completely matched my personality. In many organizations, people hesitate to customize their interactions

think · do · say

and expect the technology to do it for them. Ann's type of genuine personalization will always be more difficult and more powerful than any piece of software.

There are a host of others that inspire and inform. Sephora is so good at customization that Sailthru wrote a white paper called "Standing Up to Sephora: 6 Best Practices for Beauty Brands." Not a huge surprise given that Sephora had ranked first on Sailthru's Retail Personalization Index for the second year in a row. Walmart's personalized mobile experience and increasingly sophisticated email program is also impressive, and Amazon is redefining personalization with a robust recommendation engine that has left people realizing that Amazon knows them better than their spouse does. Nike tapped into its own data to help create over 100,000 personalized animated videos, and even Cadbury launched a "Flavor Matcher" app to match individuals with flavors of chocolate.

Your customer is a customer of one. Your client is a client of one. Your boss is a boss of one. Make sure you have the data, the insights, and the process to give them what they want.

The Most Important
Person You Do It For

I deliver a lot of keynotes, but I also lead the Think-Do-Say approach in workshop form. I get people to articulate their Brand Belief, list out who they do it for, et cetera, and they end up with their personal TDS profile. While we do each step, I get people to stand up and share their thinking with their colleagues.

One day, I was leading a workshop for over 500 employees, including everyone from the local GM to hourly paid frontline employees. When we got to, "Who do you do it for?" one guy put up his hand. I thought he was going to say, "I do it for the customer," or, "I do it for my manager." Instead, he shared a critical thought that I had completely ignored.

"No offense, brother, but I do it for myself."

He's right. The most important person you do it for is yourself. Most of us just forget it.

We make commitments to our boss without making commitments to ourselves.

We work to provide an amazing experience for our customers without pursuing an amazing experience for ourselves.

We look after people but don't look after ourselves.

We solve others' problems without addressing our own.

The most important person you do it for is yourself.

If you're not happy and fulfilled and serving yourself, you'll never truly be able to serve others.

The Second Most Important Person You Do It For

I was still in a state of amazement that I hadn't thought of "doing it for yourself" when I chose the next person to respond. He said, "I do it for my family." He was also right. There are people who depend on us to fulfill our responsibilities at work so we can fulfill our responsibilities at home. It's nice of me to write about purpose and elevating our beliefs, but sometimes in life we do what we do because we need a job, and we need to provide for our families. Food on our table will *always* be more important than any document on our desks.

We do it for ourselves.
We do it for our families.
We do it for our managers.
We do it for our clients.
We do it for our colleagues.
We do it for our partners.
We do it for Gord.

We know our Brand Belief, we have an Essential Do represented by a product or service that reinforces that belief, and we know exactly who we do it for. We could generate 400 other ideas, including big investments like buying other businesses or investing in R&D, or small investments like pizza lunches or T-shirts. I'm paid to be a creative guy, and even I'll admit that coming up with the ideas is the easy part. The challenge is prioritizing the ideas that will have the greatest impact on the audience.

You know what has the greatest impact on an audience? Meeting their needs and solving their problems. They want things from you that go beyond the functional aspects of the product you sell or the service you provide. It doesn't end with knowing who you are, it continues with what they want you to do.

DO → What Do They Want You to Do?

. . .

If there has ever been a saying that can summarize what most people who come into contact with you or your organization think, it is the brilliant line handed down from generations of consumers and middle managers:

"Shut up and solve my problem."

Yup. In a nutshell, that's the very basic element of what they want you to do. They may not say it with their outside voice, but that's what they're screaming on the inside. If they come to you, if they hire you, if they buy from you, if they manage you, if they report to you and there's an issue—they want you to just shut up. And solve their problem. That's why you're in your role and they're in theirs.

Are you a cable company people call to reconnect service?

Shut up and solve my problem.

Are you a CPG whose bottle of ketchup is hard to open?

Shut up and solve my problem.

Are you a bank that only has support during banking hours?

Shut up and solve my problem.

Are you a frontline employee, bound by procedure and unable to look at each case individually, who instead defaults to the company script, "I'm sorry, sir, but that's our policy"?

Shut up and solve my problem.

Are you an HR manager who has to advise people on their vacation and health benefits?

Shut up and solve my problem.

Are you a senior executive responsible for sorting out workplace conflict?

Shut up and solve my problem.

Coming up with the ideas is the easy part. The challenge is prioritizing the ideas that will have the greatest impact on the audience.

In a world filled with . . .

"That's not my job."

"That's against company policy."

"That's not how we do it here."

"I called but they haven't got back to me."

"We don't sell it that way."

"No, you can't unbundle the products."

"Sorry, we don't allow substitutions to the menu."

. . . shutting up and solving the person's problem is a great place to start. You don't have to be brilliant, your product doesn't have to be revolutionary, and your service doesn't have to be exceptional. This, my friends, is the lowest hurdle, and if you do it, you'll be ahead of many organizations in your category or many people in your role.

Still, this is not what people want you to do. It's what they *expect* you to do.

In this disruptive business climate, doing what people expect you to do isn't enough. To build growth in this busy, busy world, you need to do what they want you to do. And what they want you to do is to give them what they didn't even realize they wanted.

Blow It Up

Picture it. It's Friday night. You worked hard all week. You don't feel like cooking, and you desperately want to check out the new restaurant that your friends are talking about. Miraculously, you're able to get a table, so you go. The environment is cooler than anything you've seen, the ambience is young and energetic, the service is casually impeccable, the menu is original beyond belief, and the execution of every item ordered is absolutely perfect. You and your spouse enjoy a stellar meal.

Before leaving, you use the restroom and, like any civilized person over the age of six, wash your hands. You press the button on the hand dryer and realize it's one of *those* hand dryers. You know the ones. The shiny steel hand dryers with hamsters powering a small motor that slowly emits a whisper of warm air onto your hands. After seventeen minutes of rubbing under the "fan," you give up, wipe your hands on your pants, and walk out the door.

This horrible hand-drying experience has been shared by people around the globe since the hand dryer was invented. Was there *ever* a time when people didn't get frustrated and just opt for the patented wipe-and-walk? Has the hand dryer *ever* worked?

This went on for *years*. No one said a thing.

We didn't tweet about it. We didn't complain to our local news consumer watchdog. And we didn't leave a scathing Yelp review that said, "The food was amazing and the service was exceptional—but the hand dryers sucked."

Then Dyson showed up.

Inventor James Dyson was disappointed by the traditional shoddy hand dryers too. As he described in a company video, "You put your hands under the dryer, rub them a bit, then give up and wipe your hands on your trousers. We all do this." Dyson was experimenting with air blade technology and realized that it wasn't about the temperature of the air, it was about the speed. As he continued to say,

> **Instead of the old evaporation system—which blows all sorts of bacteria at you—we came up with two blades of high pressure, purified air which literally wipe off the water.**

In 2006, James Dyson delivered the Dyson Airblade to the market, and our "trousers" were saved forever. In summarizing his product, he remarked, "It's a really satisfying solution to something that's always annoyed me."

Let's hear that again.

"It's a really satisfying solution to something that's always annoyed me."

"It's a really satisfying solution to something that's always annoyed me."

Dyson tapped into the heart of that hidden frustration and created a great model for actions you can take that will make people look and will help build trust.

Satisfying solutions to things that have always annoyed people:

What do they want you to do? They want you to do *that*.

Solve the problems they were bothered by but didn't complain about. Lift your head up from your feedback surveys and think about the problems your customers, colleagues, and bosses didn't even know could be solved.

Don't Be the Thing That Always Annoys People

Whenever my car needs an oil change, I take it to a professional oil changer (is that what they're called?) because I'm a car moron. What I hate most isn't the actual oil change, it's the "after change." That's when I get requests to evaluate my oil change "experience" and grade the customer service on a scale of 1 to Ritz-Carlton. If I see one more piece of paper with "How'd we do?!" written at the top, I'm going to storm the streets.

When consumers don't like something, they have ample opportunity (and desire) to tell brands about it. Within three seconds of it happening, companies will hear about poor service issues via a tweet, an Instagram Story, a Snap, and a Facebook Live broadcast from outside their office building. Consumers are living in a world of constant expression, but brands are acting as if the only opportunity for customers to give feedback is to live in a perpetual focus group.

If your answer to, "What do they want you to do?" is, "Whatever they tell us on the feedback forms," you're not doing it correctly. Reacting to consumer complaints isn't an approach, it's a reaction. It's tough to build sustainable momentum if your customer's always ahead of you.

They don't want you to be reactive. They want you to be proactive.

Throw Away the Lock and Key

No one at Schick or Gillette realized it might be an issue that their disposable razor blades were so expensive that they were behind lock and key in local drug stores? Well, why would they? Most men (me included) didn't really rush to Twitter to rant about the price of blades. The price was the price, wasn't it? Men just collectively shrugged their shoulders, muttered, "What are you going to do?" and paid what they had to pay. What else could we do? Learn how to shave with a straight razor? Butcher our faces with the bag of plastic razors and look like we had been attacked by Edward Scissorhands?

Your customers don't want you to be reactive. They want you to be proactive.

Then Dollar Shave Club came along.

They offered quality razor blades for a buck a blade, delivered straight to your door.

Whoa. Men didn't know they wanted that because they didn't realize it was even possible. It wasn't until they had the option that they realized just how much the price of razor blades secretly annoyed them. This was *much* better than before. No schlepping to retail for something purchased every two months. No lock and key. No crazy prices. And acceptable quality. Sounds like a really satisfying solution to something that always annoyed men.

A problem isn't a problem until someone else solves it. Then, it's a huge problem.

Gillette and Schick didn't see Dollar Shave Club or Harry's coming. They were too busy competing against each other to notice that someone outside the category was gaining ground. Someone was eating their lunch (or shaving their beards), and they didn't even realize it until it was almost too late.

Start a Coup, Solve a Problem

In the 1970s, Gil Scott-Heron released the song "The Revolution Will Not Be Televised." I don't think there's a better anthem to frame the question, "What do they want you to do?" Look around. Pick a category. The real disruptors are the ones who are solving the problems the establishment can't or won't. Usually, that disruption is accompanied by the phrase, "Huh. Where did that come from?"

The revolution will not be televised.

Many of you reading this book are members of the establishment. You're in an established organization with an established role, established procedures, established compensation, and established language, all laddering up to an established business model that your direct competition adheres to as well. You go to association conferences—which should really be called "a gathering of the establishment"—where you share the same approaches using the same success stories by the same people. You know one another, you network with one another, and you protect one another. The problems you talk about fixing are reactionary feedback problems. You can't see the forest because you've been trained to fix the trees.

As the establishment:

1. There are problems you won't solve

When James Dyson created the first bagless vacuum, he pitched the invention to the establishment—the major vacuum manufacturers in the UK. He solved a problem that always annoyed people (the bag), but the establishment didn't want to touch it because they made millions every year from selling the bags. They wouldn't solve the problem because they would lose revenue. In the end, they lost revenue all right. Dyson manufactured the bagless vacuum himself, and within three years it became the number-one vacuum in the UK. There are problems the establishment won't solve because their business model is rooted in the problem itself.

2. There are problems you can't solve

Competing with start-ups is not exactly a level playing field. Established organizations have shareholders and fiduciary responsibilities. Most start-ups don't even need to show a profit because investors give them time to perfect their model. Shareholders are impatient and want a return. VCs are patient and want to cash out. There's a big difference between the two. And start-ups have foosball!

It's easy to say that Schick and Gillette should be like Harry's and Dollar Shave Club. Sure, they could have done a *lot* of things to bring down the price of their blades, but flipping the switch on their entire business model to abandon retail, destroy relationships, establish new methods of distribution, and train an entire (smaller) workforce is a tad more challenging. There are problems the establishment can't solve because, sometimes, it's easier to build a ship than to turn one around.

I was with some CEOs from some of the largest global organizations for a speaking event, where one CEO from a global e-commerce company heaped praise on the CEO of a massive and successful brick-and-mortar retailer. His praise was simple:

> Building a business like I did has its challenges. But it's a
> hell of a lot easier than turning one around like [he] did.

It's easier to come up with a revolutionary idea to topple the establishment when you're not a part of it. Business disruptors are usually from the outside, so they're not entrenched in how it's "normally done." They're not obsessed with benchmarking the competition, and they're not focused on hiring only people with experience in the industry. Pick a category and you'll probably find a disruptor taking down (or at least putting a serious dent into) the competition.

No one saw Uber coming.
No one saw Square coming.
No one saw Airbnb coming.
No one saw WeWork coming.
No one saw Red Bull coming.
The revolution will not be televised.

It's easier to come up with a revolutionary idea to topple the establishment when you're not a part of it.

We're not seeing disruption in business. We're seeing a coup of the establishment.

Like a political coup, insurgent business forces topple the establishment when the establishment spends more time protecting its position than earning its position. Before long, new voices emerge, promising to give people what they really want. In the dead of night, when no one expects it, they storm the castle, take out the leaders, and insert themselves on the throne.

Donald Trump didn't win an election. It was a coup of the establishment.

He was from outside the category. No one saw him coming.

He toppled the old guard by promising really satisfying solutions to something that had always annoyed his base (immigration, trade, political correctness).

The revolution will not be televised.

Netflix didn't "beat" Blockbuster. It was a coup of the home entertainment establishment.

They came from outside the category. No one saw them coming.

They toppled the old guard (not just Blockbuster, but all video stores) by providing a really satisfying solution to something that had always annoyed people (late fees, limited selection, limited access).

Want people to look in your direction? Start solving their real problems before someone else does.

think · do · say

Storm the Castle
from within the Castle

Start-ups are sexy. There, I said it.

They are. They're rebellious. They're informal. They believe that solving the problem is more important than solving the business model. And like it or not, there is something attractive about the idea of working your ass off for a few years and surviving the emotional highs and lows so you can exit with generational wealth. Yeah, start-ups are kinda cool.

Well... at least the successful ones are. The unsuccessful ones are to be concealed and ignored as if they're the Elephant Man of the business world.

We have an epidemic: the celebration of the start-up as the only viable path to wealth for young people. They're bowing down in front of the Zuckerberg altar, they're misquoting scripture from Gary Vaynerchuk about the hustle and the grind, and they have a greater appreciation for Jack Dorsey than Jack Welch. My LinkedIn feed is filled with young business VJs sharing daily videos that dole out advice on making it in the business world even though they don't appear to have a business that makes anything but the video itself.

Let me (possibly) be the first to say it: there's nothing wrong with a J-O-B.

We have an epidemic: the celebration of the start-up as the only viable path to wealth for young people.

There are thousands of organizations that have already done what start-ups are trying to do. They started, they grew, they went public, and they still make a *lot* of money for a *lot* of people. They optimized their production, smoothed out operations, and rid themselves of the chaos that accompanies a coup. They stormed the castle, they got the T-shirt, and they're doing very well, thank you very much.

I'm willing to bet that's most of you reading this book.

You don't work for a twelve-person start-up operating out of a garage, eating pizza at midnight, getting nothing but sweat equity in return for trying to disrupt the "knitting space." You work at a desk in a large office tower with reasonable hours, good benefits, good compensation, and a one-drink-ticket holiday party once a year. Someone associated with your company was, at some point, a rebel. They struck out on their own, they made something out of nothing, and now, years later, you and your colleagues benefit from their sacrifice.

Just don't forget that staying in power is often far more difficult than taking it.

Your role, should you choose to accept it, is to perform a series of ongoing coups from within the castle walls. Wouldn't you rather disrupt your company than be toppled by a kid with a good idea and Series A financing?

When you do it, just one thing, K? Please. Please. Please. Don't act like a start-up.

"Big companies should act like a start-up" is one of the laziest and least effective pieces of advice told to members of the establishment. Please don't. A large, established organization trying to act like a start-up always reminds me of Amy Poehler's character in *Mean Girls*. "I'm not like the other moms . . . I'm a cool mom." You're a grown up. Act like it.

You have experience, expertise, infrastructure, customers, and, usually, profit. Use that to your advantage. Here's how.

Assembly Line versus Concept Car

You should have two parts to your business and career. Just act like an automotive manufacturer.

1. The assembly line

In the delivery of your Essential Do, there is a series of activities done in succession that generate a "thing" at the end of an assembly line. The assembly line is where your profit comes from because every single ounce of inefficiency has been removed. Everyone's roles are very clearly defined and their actions are repeatable, so when they're executed the same way every single time, quality is maintained, costs are contained, and the margin is

Just don't forget that staying in power is often far more difficult than taking it.

consistent. There's no collaboration on the assembly line. Everyone does their job, they pass it off to the next person, and the line continues with peak efficiency. What ad agencies say when something needs to go on the assembly line is, "Kill it and bill it." Put your head down. Get it done. And move on to the next task.

2. The concept car

When automotive manufacturers want to explore new ideas to topple their own established ways of thinking, they create a concept car. The concept car is off the assembly line. There's no hope or expectation that the concept car will ever go into production. The car folks just do it to see what they can learn. Sometimes, they'll discover that one component of the concept car can be integrated into the assembly line. Over time, the assembly line innovates responsibly because of the experimental components that feed it.

The assembly line is where you make your money.

The concept car is where you spend your money.

Most start-ups are just building concept cars. Most established organizations are just assembly lines. The best type of organization is the one that can have a healthy balance of the two.

Some additional thoughts to consider:

1   With intense pressure to innovate, many organiza-
    tions are trying to build multiple concept cars in the
    middle of the assembly line. The result is absolute
    chaos. No one is exactly sure what they're supposed
    to do or how their success will be evaluated, and
    morale craters over the uncertainty. There's no repeat-
    able behavior, so quality goes down, costs go up, and
    margin is eroded. The result is that the skeptics take
    a look at the numbers and grumble, "I told you we
    should have just done it the old way."

2   The first step to innovation is improving the efficiency
    of what you already do. There are things that you do
    as an individual that can be done far more efficiently
    than you do them right now. Remember Management
    by Reply-All? Many of you are trying to inspire your
    teams by writing Outlook novellas and then, surprise,
    there's no time at the end of the day to try something
    new. Get efficient. Then start exploring.

3   I was in a group conversation with the famous CEO of
    a global disruptor at the previously mentioned event.
    When talking about innovation, he pointed out the
    difficulty of developing "concept cars" for established
    organizations. When a start-up has a great idea, they
    can pitch twenty VCs in a row, getting a "no" every
    time. But if the twenty-first VC says yes, they can go

Most start-ups are just building concept cars. Most established organizations are just assembly lines. The best type of organization is the one that can have a healthy balance of the two.

to market. Within large organizations, if someone has a great concept car, they have to pitch the idea up a long line of bosses and get a "yes" every single time. The first "no" they encounter kills the idea. Individuals have to remove self-doubt to pursue personal concept cars.

4 I don't love the phrase "embrace failure" because there are times when we should definitely *not* embrace failure. At no point should you embrace failure on the assembly line. There is no room for failure there. You've done it a million times, and anything that veers from repeatable behavior is not to be embraced. Failure should be embraced only on things that you've never done before. Concept car failure should be expected and accepted. Assembly-line failure should be penalized.

Take great pride in being the establishment. Your skills and goals may be different than those of the insurgents, but they're just as valuable. Use your position of power to truly make life better for those you serve. If you do, they'll serve you back with loyalty. Storm the castle from within the castle.

Light your torches. Start marching for progress. Lead the coup.

You can make your business great again. You just need to know who you're marching with.

DO → Who Do You Do It With?

. . .

My grandfather, Nicandro Vocino, was an entrepreneur—but not in the way that we think of entrepreneurs today. He wasn't the Italian version of Mark Zuckerberg or Elon Musk. He didn't wear a hoodie and Allbirds, he didn't have his own Instagram account, and he didn't launch his idea on *Shark Tank*. He wasn't a disruptor and he didn't take down the establishment.

He started a business that was a response to "Shut up and solve my problem," but the problem was his.

He had to feed his family.

Grampa moved from Italy when he was in his teens. Almost immediately, he began working in the shoe repair business. One day, after he was married and had started a family, he was pulled aside by his boss and informed that the business was going to be sold and that he was probably going to lose his job.

There was only one solution to the dilemma.

To guarantee his own employment, my grandfather had to be the one to buy the business.

He had no money. He had no connections. And getting VC dollars for a shoe repair retail business wasn't in the cards. So he did the only thing he could do. He surrounded himself with partners with whom he shared values, called in some favors, promised absolute loyalty, and lived up to it.

He had to go to the bank and beg for money. His collateral was his word. He made two promises to the bank. He would work 24/7 until he paid back the loan and he would bank with that financial institution for as long as the business was open.

The bank loaned him the money.

Next, he needed leather, glue, tacks, and other supplies, but couldn't pay for them until he got money for fixing the shoes. It was the first step of cash flow, a chicken-and-egg kind of thing. So, he went to a supplier and asked to be fronted the supplies. In return, my grandfather promised his loyalty. "If you help me out, I will always buy my supplies from you," he said.

The leather and glue company gave him the supplies he needed to get started on a deferred payment plan.

My grandfather had the business for over sixty years.

He bought his supplies from the same company the entire time.

My grandfather lived until he was ninety-nine.

He banked with the same financial institution until the day he died.

The two organizations weren't officially a part of the business, but they were aligned with it on values of trust and integrity. They weren't on my grandfather's payroll, but they were as much a part of the company as any assistant was. My grandfather's customers didn't know who they were, but their involvement was almost as important to the customer experience as anything my grandfather did.

It didn't matter what he called them.
It didn't matter what he paid them.
It didn't matter where they were located.

The people you do it *for*—especially in a retail environment—will always come and go, but the people and companies you do it *with* can be with you forever because you're aligned on purpose and values.

Choose "With" over "For"

Selling out a partner is not only morally corrupt, it's also a disservice to all the future clients who would benefit from their involvement.

Who you do it with is more important than who you do it for.

Thanks to the gig economy, we have more partners, vendors, suppliers, freelancers, and people on contract than ever before. Because organizations have outsourced

Who you do
it with is more
important
than who you
do it for.

many aspects of their business, the different types of people we do it with are growing. They're not on our payroll, but they all came from the same budget.

As an organization:
Who you do it with can help you serve all your clients.
Who you do it with can help you be more efficient.
Who you do it with can be specialists in an area that you don't have to develop.

You also have people in your individual network who allow you to do the things you really want to do and the things you're really good at. There are people in your network who exist both inside and outside your organization who contribute in some way to your success.

Who you do it with can be the one who supports you. Or inspires you. Or informs you.

Or protects you. Or promotes you.

I often lead an exercise with organizations where individuals think about others in the organization who help them achieve success. Then, I get them to approach and tell those people why what they do is so important.

Sometimes, it's functional.

"Sam. You take care of the gas and I take care of the windows, and together we provide great service."

Sometimes, it's stress relief.

"Tammy, when the job becomes really stressful, I know that you will make me laugh. I get through the day because of you."

Sometimes, it's educational.

"Sheila, when I don't know what to do, you know because of your experience."

Sometimes, it's emotional.

"Tom, you have always had my back, and I only hope that my own loyalty can repay you."

I've seen people laugh and cry and every appropriate professional response in between, but the one thing I see most often is from the people being told they're important to someone else: surprise.

They don't know they're important.
They don't know they're appreciated.
They don't know they're even noticed.
That's sad, isn't it?

Who you do it with is more important than who you do it for. But you need to tell them about it. We have to acknowledge, recognize, thank, and protect who we do it with.

Who helps you succeed?

And when was the last time you thanked them?

Thank them now.

The Power of Partnership

There are people and companies who complete your operations by providing a function that you need in order to be in business. Maybe it's a distribution company that delivers your product to retail. Or a janitorial service that cleans your offices. Or an agency that provides creative services. They may be outside vendors, but they should feel like they're inside colleagues. After all, they don't have to be on the payroll to be on the team.

There are also those who may not be critical to your operations but who are critical because they complement your offering and help you take it to the next level. You do the same for them. You need them. They need you. This complement is important when you try something for the first time. Sure, unique product offerings and one-of-a-kind experiences may help get people to look because people rubberneck to see something they've never seen before.

There's a downside, though. New stuff may capture consumers' attention, but it rarely builds trust. How does one trust something they've never experienced before? They're left thinking, "That's cool. But will I like it?" Or, "Wow. That's really interesting, but will it work?"

People need to know where to look and who to trust.

If it's new, they'll look but they may not trust.

Collaborations with partners who share your beliefs can generate unique products and promotions. Establishing trust can be accelerated by the presence of a brand that brings credibility.

If it's old, they'll trust but they won't necessarily look.

I think this is called a "catch-22," but I've never read the book (I know, I know...), so I'll just say, "Man, you're damned if you do and damned if you don't."

Unless, that is, you can find a partner who can either add trust and credibility to your new offering or add a unique and compelling offering that extends your trust.

That's when who you do it *with* allows you to provide something that speaks directly to who you do it *for*, and directly addresses what they want you to do.

Here's a quick example.

Butter chicken isn't something one normally sees at the quick-service restaurant Pita Pit. Typically served on rice with naan bread on the side, butter chicken is not usually shoved inside a pita with grilled vegetables, lettuce, and the secret sauce, and served up in an environment that doesn't exactly scream "Mumbai."

If Pita Pit wanted to sell a butter chicken pita, it would probably be unique enough to get people to look. But would consumers trust it? Would they really believe that Pita Pit had the cultural credibility to pull off a tasty and authentic Indian dish when there is nothing in their history to indicate that they could?

They could. They did.

That's because we worked with Pita Pit on behalf of one of our clients, Patak's, the leading Indian culinary brand in Canada.

During Diwali, Pita Pit offered a Patak's–branded butter chicken pita, and it became a perfect partnership. Patak's contributed authentic Indian heritage and a delicious sauce, while Pita Pit brought preparation, distribution, and a proven sales channel. Even if they had created an amazing butter chicken sauce themselves, it would have taken Pita Pit a long time to convince the consumer they could be trusted. And if Patak's had set up pop-up shops during Diwali across North America, it would have been impossible to establish the process and network needed to get the dish to market in the time they did.

Collaborations with partners who share your beliefs can generate unique products and promotions. Establishing trust can be accelerated by the presence of a brand that brings credibility.

Pita Pit did it with Patak's.

Patak's did it with Pita Pit.

Consumers saw it. Consumers trusted it. Consumers bought it.

Words and Pictures

Just as your company may rely on other organizations to complement your capabilities, there may be individuals who complement yours.

I've certainly had my share.

In advertising, the traditional creative team has been a copywriter and an art director. One looks after words (lines, copy, scripts) while the other looks after the visuals (colors, fonts, photography, design). Together they generate creative concepts.

Over my career, I've been fortunate to have been teamed up with some brilliant art directors. Each relationship was different, but what was consistent was that we acted as a team. We protected our partners. We supported our partners. We looked out for our partners.

Who we did it with was more important than who we did it for.

Who I did it with was both an absolute necessity (I had no idea how to use Photoshop or Illustrator and had limited talent as an art director) and an emotional necessity. Being creative is tough. When you're working from a blank page, generating new ideas that have never been tested before and setting yourself up for possible embarrassment and failure, you need to know that *someone* has your back. Who has yours?

When we moved into the concept's execution, our creative partnership expanded to include people who worked outside our organization. We looped in directors, producers, audio engineers, musicians, actors, editors, and more. They weren't full-time members of the team, and we called on different people for specific tasks, but we were always aligned on the goals and the purpose of the work. We didn't care about titles and we didn't care about protecting turf. And while we cared about money, we let other people worry about it and rarely let it get in the way of doing an amazing job. If we had to call in a favor from you on one job, we'd get you on the next one.

It's a shame, but once the accountants took over and started to nickel-and-dime every line item on a production budget, this type of collaboration stopped. I don't like asking for favors that I can't pay back. Creatives stopped being able to protect their outside partners, and the result has been a disaster. The work has suffered. The relationships have suffered. The business has suffered.

Who we do it with has changed.

The large multinationals forced the change when they tried to apply spreadsheet thinking to creative collaboration, and in the process they trampled on the very structure that was built to generate great work for them. They destroyed relationships that were formed for them and their business.

Hey, multinationals, how'd that work out? Whose lunch is getting eaten by faster, leaner, and more creative start-ups?

Box It Up

I hear a lot of superficial talk from senior executives encouraging their staff to innovate.

"We need to be creative," they'll say. "We need to do stuff that has never been done before! We need to embrace failure. We need to think outside the box."

That hall-of-fame jargon again. I think there's something hilarious about requesting new and innovative thinking by using one of the most over-used, clichéd, stale expressions of the modern age. It's like saying, "We gotta be cutting-edge cool!" while exposing your barbed-wire bicep tattoo.

Furthermore, saying they'll embrace failure may make them sound like contemporary leaders, but the expression gets discounted when they don't support it by changing compensation systems, performance review methodology, and President's Club criteria. Usually when I pull back the covers, I don't find organizations that embrace failure. I find leaders who punish it.

When someone is really passionate about a new idea, they're not usually worried about professional failure,

Usually when I pull back the covers, I don't find organizations that embrace failure. I find leaders who punish it.

they're worried about emotional failure. They're not worried about getting fired. They're worried about getting laughed at.

Reprimands, poor performance reviews, and constructive feedback are all private. But the ridicule that follows dumb ideas is public. They can get over a negative review, but they'll never lose the feeling in the pit of their stomach of "that one time in that meeting when I suggested that thing that was so stupid."

Getting to the one brilliant idea requires generating five crappy ideas and talking about the bad ones out loud. Crappy ideas have to be poked and prodded and improved and reshaped and crumpled up and pulled apart so that the brilliant ideas can emerge.

I have never done my best and most fulfilling work with the people who discussed great ideas. I did it with the people with whom I felt most comfortable discussing horrible ideas. When your mind is so open that you feel safe suggesting something ridiculously stupid, brilliant ideas are around the corner.

Who Has Your Back?

For five glorious years, I was the host and one of the executive producers of Monkey Toast, a hit comedy show in Toronto. Originally created by the great David Shore, Monkey Toast combines compelling conversation with brilliant comedy, delivered by a cast of improvisers, many of whom are alumni of The Second City.

As host, I'd interview a special guest who could be a politician, a celebrity, a musician, a surgeon, or someone from some other interesting profession. We'd have a serious but light conversation before I'd pause with, "Let's stop right there and let's see some comedy." Then, the cast would improvise scenes based on the discussion that *just* took place. They'd create hilarious characters, songs, and more right there on the spot without knowing anything in advance. They heard it for the first time when the audience heard it for the first time.

To put it in perspective, that's like your CEO calling your team in for an impromptu meeting, giving you a product you've never seen, and asking you to present a detailed launch strategy, complete with creative and budgets, all without the opportunity to confer first.

As you can imagine, that type of teamwork requires more than an off-site T-shirt ("Team Building Exercise '99!") and a ropes course. It requires trust.

Before every show, without fail, the cast would huddle up and perform a ritual that is echoed by the casts of The Second City and others in the improv community. After discussing the show and welcoming our special guests, every cast member—including host, musical director, stage manager, and lighting and sound crew—would connect with every other cast member, look them in the eye, pat them on the back, and simultaneously say, "I've got your back." Just as the doors were closing and the show was about to start, there was the beautiful sound of pairs saying, "I've got your back . . . I've got your back . . . I've got your back . . ."

Even just thinking of it makes me tear up, fondly recollecting the special bond I had with the cast of Monkey Toast. See, they knew something that more business people need to learn: if you're going to attempt to do something that has never been done before, taking the risk is easier and more fulfilling when you know that you have a practical and emotional support network behind you.

Someone has to have your back. And you have to have theirs.

If you want to do great work . . .
If you want to get people to look up . . .
If you want people to trust you . . .
If you want to solve problems . . .

If you want to generate positive momentum for you and your organization, you're going to need someone to do it with.

What you may not realize is that—for someone inside or outside your organization—you're that person.

Keep it up.

(If you got the "Team Building Exercise '99" reference, email me at ron@churchstate.co, OK? The first one to get it and the 100th one to get it will each win a free bundle of business books.)

"People say, 'Put your money where your mouth is.' Nope. I say, 'Put your foot where you mouth is. I'm sick of hearing all the crap from your yap.'"

THE DALAI LAMA

THIS IS THE SAY PART

Words matter.
Phrases matter.
Terms matter.
Descriptions
matter.

Creating Wealth Is Simple

. . .

We open on a beach.

The sun is shining. The waves are . . . what *do* waves actually do? Do they lap? Sure. OK. Then the waves are lapping. Complementing the beach sounds is an acoustic music track featuring a ukulele. A lens flare hits the camera. A married couple enter the frame carrying surfboards. Before heading in to crash the waves, they turn to the camera with big massive grins to communicate, "You're on a couch. And we're surfing the waves in a tropical location in the middle of February. Ain't life wonderful?"

The married couple is over sixty years old.

Thankfully, they planned their retirement with the financial institution that funded this production and that paid its agency to crank out the lowest common denominator retirement savings pre-roll creative. It doesn't really matter who it is. It could be any financial institution. If it's not a surfboard, it's a scooter. If it's not a scooter, it's a snowboard. Yawn.

Retirement is actually pretty scary. One or two key decisions could determine whether you retire to a beach in Florida or a rented trailer in Fredericton (Nothing against Fredericton, I just needed an "F"). But no one ever says that, do they? Nope. Most financial institutions lead consumer-targeted financial discussions in the same way: hyper-positive, don't worry about a thing, here's a bunch of numbers that will sound great along with some complex industry jargon so just . . . you know . . . trust us . . . and you can be like these happy surfing people.

How can you trust an organization that talks about their products by reading the same overwritten script as their competition with no personality, no unique language, and no dialogue that's actually based in reality? It's not like they're a part of an industry that created a financial crisis. Oh, wait. They are.

When consumers don't know where to look, using the same complex and impersonal script as everyone else won't get them to look. When consumers don't know who to trust, a jargon-filled conversation that talks above their head doesn't build it.

Enter Wealthsimple.

Launched in 2014, Wealthsimple is an alternative online investment service known as a "robo-advisor" (like *RoboCop* with calculators) that invests their clients' money in low-cost index funds.

Wealthsimple doesn't use a Brand Belief, but I think theirs would be, "We believe a sound financial future should be accessible for all." Everything they do makes investing easy. They have no minimum account balance. They have low fees. They're available everywhere (online). They have a really easy registration process.

Finally, their purpose and actions are great, but Wealthsimple's biggest competitive advantage is their SAY. In a sea of surfboards promising the world, they take a different approach.

It's not just what is said, it's how it's said, and who it's said by.

Who's Saying the SAY?

Let's face it, what most banks show to the world is stale, pale, and male. If it's not always an old gray-haired white dude talking about his retirement, it sure seems that way. Watch Wealthsimple's advertising and right away, you realize that these are the people who never get shown talking about money. There are women, people of color, young people, fashionable people, and quirky people. In other words, real people. Shockingly, real people like to hear from real people.

How Are They Saying It?

Wealthsimple doesn't just make investing accessible through their product. They also make it accessible through language and tone. How they say things—with unique and authentic personality, imperfect and natural dialogue, laughter, and even tears—is so natural that consumers look up. They earn trust because they don't try to sound perfect (when we all know no one is).

What Are They Saying?

Wealthsimple rarely leads with numbers, financial performance, or product attributes. They put purpose before product and they do that through the content of the dialogue. They talk about things that no one *ever* talks about in financial services. They openly discuss the pain of money. The challenge of money. The emotions behind money.

"Money was something that you weren't supposed to talk about..."

"But when you watch the economy crash as you enter the workforce..."

"There was no money to save..."

They don't just talk about what money allows us to do (go surfing!), they talk about what it causes us to do (worry, cry, feel dumb). As I mentioned earlier, there's no better reason to look up than, "I've never heard this before."

A summary of Wealthsimple's SAY, and a line that can direct a unique and compelling SAY for all of you, is in the last and most important line from one of their spots:

> **If people were talking more openly about money, it would be better, right?**

You can apply that approach to any category, any organization, any situation, and the result would be getting people to look and getting people to trust.

If people were talking more openly about car repair, it would be better, right?

If people were talking more openly about office politics, it would be better, right?

If people were talking more openly about marriage, it would be better, right?

If people were talking more openly about their fears, it would be better, right?

Yes. It would all be better. You just have to say it that way.

Say the SAY

. . .

If you have a Brand Belief *and* you act in ways that reinforce it, well, that is worth talking about, and consumers won't feel pitch slapped when you do. But if you *are* going to talk about it, you should make conscious choices so that you get as many people looking and trusting as possible. When you have the permission to communicate, you need the desire to communicate effectively.

Like Wealthsimple, you and your organization should focus on:

1 What to say
2 How to say it

Doing so contributes to building personal and organizational momentum. It would be a shame if people and organizations were incredibly disciplined in what they believed and what they did but then provided no guidance to their people on communicating it all.

SAY → What to Say

Be an Action Figure

With Barbies flying off the shelf in the early 1960s, struggling Hasbro thought little boys could use their own masculine and heroic products to play with. They wanted to make dolls for boys.

So in 1964, they launched G.I. Joe.

Hasbro's THINK and DO may have been, "We believe that little boys need male role models as inspiration SO we created a fictional doll soldier they can play with" (which sounds great), but even Hasbro knew that no one was going to buy them if they called them dolls. Dudes weren't exactly wearing salmon polos or throwing around the term "metrosexual" in the '60s. Men were men. And only girls played with dolls.

So they called the new toys "action figures."

Those were the words that communicated the combination of what the brand believed and what they did to reinforce that belief. During that era, the word "doll" would have contradicted the masculine nature of their beliefs and the rugged exterior of their products.

G.I. Joe needed that specific SAY to be successful, and if that's what was needed, it was critical that everyone used the term at every single touch point.

When you have
the permission
to communicate,
you need
the desire to
communicate
effectively.

Hasbro understood this, internally prohibited the use of the word "doll," and wouldn't sell through any retailer that disagreed.

While this strategy might not be appropriate for today, it was needed at the time. As you probably know, it worked. Within two years of launch, G.I. Joe drove 66 percent of Hasbro's revenue.

If you read this book and commit to taking actions that reinforce your belief, you shouldn't refer to yourself as an executive or a middle manager. You should call yourself an "action figure."

The words organizations choose to label, define, and describe their products can be the difference between people looking up and people looking away. No one would have looked up for a "boy's doll," and no one would have trusted an organization that had chosen to launch one.

When Uber was fighting municipal policymakers around the world, they were very careful with the language they used to describe themselves. Their detractors called them a "transportation" company and, because of it, found them to be an illegal operation who failed to have the necessary transportation licenses to operate. Uber disagreed and said they were a technology company that didn't need to adhere to transportation requirements. Had they not made that specific choice, I doubt Uber would still exist.

This is the reason why my friend Phil M. Jones wrote the best-selling book, *Exactly What to Say: The Magic Words for Influence and Impact*. Phil knows that to drive influence and impact, specific phrases can be the difference between success and failure. Specific words can be the difference between someone taking your call and someone letting it go to voice mail. WHAT you say can be the difference between people choosing to snurf or not.

You'll understand what that means in 3 . . . 2 . . . 1 . . .

Is "Snurf" a Smurf?

Everyone thinks that Jake Burton invented snowboarding in 1977. I will give him this: Jake is the main reason snowboarding is as popular as it is. He didn't just build a company or a sport, he built an entire culture. It wasn't easy, either. The ski resorts didn't want it. The skiers certainly didn't want it. Even the ski equipment manufacturers didn't want snowboarding to succeed. Luckily, Jake was committed to helping people surf on snow, and eventually he prevailed.

But he didn't invent it.

In 1966, Sherman Poppen invented a very similar device. After making a couple of prototypes for his kids, he continually improved the design and sold it to Brunswick. By 1970, a million units had been sold. Impressive.

So why does Jake Burton get all the credit?

Well, that's because Sherman Poppen didn't call the sport "snowboarding."

He called it "snurfing."

Yeah. You read that right. The coolest sport invented in the last fifty years sounds like it was originally named after a forgotten Muppet. The activity that invented such weed-inspired terms as "goofy," "boned out," and "steezy" once used a piece of equipment that was called a "Snurfer."

In fact, Burton only called the sport snowboarding out of necessity. He originally called his product a snurf board, but Poppen claimed the name was too close to his Snurfer trademark and threatened legal action, so Burton changed the name to snowboard. Poppen's device did a faceplant. Burton's did a Stiffy-Air Half-Cab McTwist followed by a Tail Poke.

Words matter.
Phrases matter.
Terms matter.
Descriptions matter.

The coolest sport invented in the last fifty years sounds like it was originally named after a forgotten Muppet.

WHAT you say matters, and you may have to go through 500 versions before you get it right. You may even need to bring in communication specialists from outside your organization before you finally land on the exact words you use in your SAY.

When you get it right—whether it's your email signature, your proprietary real estate selling technique, or even the name of your company—what you say can determine whether people understand what you believe and what you do.

When companies get it right—whether it's the name of their boardrooms, the internal posters on the wall, or the taglines under their logo—what they say determines whether people buy into the brand or tune out of the message.

What you say can bring you success.

It can also help you avoid catastrophe.

Get Your Life Back

Have you ever heard of the Transocean Oil Spill? No? It was rather huge. A Transocean oil rig blew up in the Gulf of Mexico. Eleven people died. Over 3 million barrels of oil leaked into the Gulf. It was the largest marine oil spill in the history of the world. You didn't hear about it?

Oh. Wait. You probably heard about it by its other, more common name: The BP Oil Disaster.

Transocean owned the oil rig that blew up. Of the eleven people who sadly died in the accident, nine were Transocean employees. So, if it was their rig that blew up and it was their people who perished, why isn't it known as the "Transocean Disaster"? It's because sometimes what we say isn't the difference that allows us to succeed, it's the difference that prevents us from failing. What we say can help drive personal or organizational momentum, but it can also protect us from Integrity Gaps.

Before I go any further, I should clarify something: I'm not trying to make light of a horrible event, and even though I'm adding perspective on a very specific detail, the *only* important part of the disaster is that eleven dedicated and hard-working innocent people died that day, and our planet suffered irreparable harm. No post-explosion SAY will ever be as important as the pre-explosion DOs that should have been done by everyone involved.

I'm merely pointing out that one organization's name is front and center and bears the brunt of the public disgust, and one organization's name is unknown to most casual observers. The reason why is the communications strategy that immediately followed.

Transocean hired FTI Consulting. (Full disclosure: I was hired as a speaker for FTI five years in a row. It's where I first heard the story.) Transocean, under the advisement of FTI, did three things really well in crafting their response.

1   They were fast. They started connecting with media immediately. They had to say something, and they started communicating as quickly as they could. As FTI writes, "Remember: Not telling your story gives others license to tell it for you." (And by "story," they don't mean a fictional account. WHAT you say shouldn't contain anything but the truth.)

2   They were consistent. With so many different audiences, what they said to one group had to be consistent with what they were telling the others. Once you have WHAT you say, say that every time.

3   The third thing that Transocean did was more about their actions: They acted and spoke with empathy. Their CEO visited the families of the victims. They held a memorial service. After such a horrific tragedy, they reacted with warmth.

Transocean knew specifically what to say and said it consistently. BP, on the other hand ... After catastrophic events killed eleven people and did irreversible damage to the Gulf of Mexico and its wildlife, after thousands worked around the clock to stop and contain the leak, after local fisherman were devastated, BP CEO Tony Hayward complained, "I'd like my life back."

What you say is pretty damn important.

How do you want to be remembered?

Swindle Speak

In its absolute simplest form, WHAT you say is pretty easy. You should just say:

1 What you believe
2 The relevant and specific actions you take to reinforce that belief

That's it.

"We believe that a life lived outside is a life worth living, so we're going to close on Black Friday so our staff can be in the mountains instead of the aisles."

Of course, HOW you say it needs to be unique and authentic, and as you've just read, the specific words you use to communicate should be chosen very carefully.

But the intent of what you say should be focused on only those two things.

Here's the problem. I know exactly what's going to happen: People are going to game the system. They're going to cheat. They're going to take the easy way out. They're going to jump right to the SAY and hope that the beliefs and actions follow. It's the software company that creates a commercial and hopes the product lives up to it. It's the CEO who calls a layoff "restructuring" so she can avoid saying what she doesn't want to. It's the interior designer who talks about what he wants to do instead of what he routinely does.

One of the most frustrating places I see this is in job titles. It's laughable, really.

When faced with an internal engagement issue and huge morale problem, I've witnessed organizations decide to *not* do the heavy lifting required to solve the problem, but instead just change the titles of people.

Those who are unhappy with opportunities for promotion are suddenly made VPs even though their compensation, responsibilities, and direct reports all stay the same. That's Swindle Speak.

After being called out for unfair practices and hearing complaints from their vendors, senior management decides that, moving forward, all vendors will be referred to as "partners," even though their idea of partnership is rather one-sided. "These prices are too high. Come on, we're partners!" That's Swindle Speak.

But that's nothing compared to the CFO. The CFO makes my blood boil. The CFO makes me roll my eyes faster than a possessed child in a 1980s horror flick. Nothing loses my respect faster than the CFO.

I'm not talking about the chief financial officer. No, I'm talking about the situation when morale is so low that some brainiac decides to hand out non-traditional titles. Instead of companies improving compensation, listening to employees, overhauling the office layout, and revolutionizing reporting structure, everyone now goes by the title CFO: chief fun officer.

Want to improve engagement in your organization? Screw consultants. Just tell everyone that their title is chief fun officer and your job is over.

That's Swindle Speak.

What you say works only when it clearly articulates what you believe and what you do. If it represents an aspirational state—where you'd like to be—as opposed to a realistic state—where you actually are—you may get people to look, but you won't get them to trust.

SAY → How to Say It

F-Bombs Away

The rebel and philosopher George Carlin had a lot of brilliant comedy in his career, but the most famous is probably "Seven Words You Can Never Say on Television," a bit he first performed on his 1972 comedy album, *Class Clown*.

> Yeah. There are 400,000 words in the English language and there are seven of them you can't say on television. What a ratio that is!

Now, you don't need me to go through the seven words. If you don't know them, just hit your thumb with a hammer and you'll probably scream five of them in a row.

As Carlin indirectly pointed out, those seven words were "the heavy seven. Those are the ones that'll infect your soul, curve your spine, and keep the country from winning the war."

As nutty as it may sound now, during that time, Carlin was right. TV was the epitome of the communication establishment. If you wanted to join it, either as an advertiser or in programming, there were formal and

More and
more, informal
language
is building
trust, not
destroying it.

informal rules that governed your language. At the time, those seven specific words were considered offensive and highly inappropriate not just for TV but for society in general. Carlin actually got arrested for disturbing the peace in Milwaukee after performing the bit live.

Swearing and cursing were frowned upon in life, and certainly at work. Organizations built trust by showing that they were a part of the establishment, by looking and acting like everyone else. Gosh darn it, there was a script to follow, and anyone or any company that veered from it was considered countercultural and was not to be trusted. The '60s may have created the hippie movement, but business—and certainly business communications— was still filled with a bunch of Ward Cleavers.

Oh, what a different time we live in now.

We went from the seven words you could never say on television to Dollar Shave Club's launch video that proudly exclaimed, "Our blades are fucking great."

That's the exact opposite of the golly-gee era that Carlin ranted against. Dollar Shave Club founder Michael Dubin, who was once a part of the Second City– like Upright Citizens Brigade in New York, used the tone of his language to distance himself from the establish- ment. The existing ruling class charged exorbitant fees for blades with unnecessary features and sold them at retail, an outdated and inefficient distribution method. His entire business model, a buck a blade delivered straight to your door, was built on contradicting their business model—so the content and tone of his language had to contradict theirs, too.

More and more, informal language is building trust, not destroying it. Unscripted language with imperfections built right in is considered more authentic. Have you taken a look at your bookstore recently?

The Subtle Art of Not Giving a Fuck
You Are a Badass
Fuck You Very Much
The Joy of Leaving Your Shit All Over the Place
Get Your Shit Together

Are we writing books or are we participating in an F-bomb contest?

Even Kraft Mac & Cheese ("KD" in Canada) brought in Melissa Mohr, a swearing expert and author of *Holy Shit: A Brief History of Swearing*. Representing one of the most mass-marketed products in the world, she proudly told the 26 percent of parents who claimed that they had never sworn in front of their children that they were full of shit. The 1:35 brand video has fourteen curse words (bleeped out).

It's not just on the screen or in print, either. Conference event planners are reminding hired comedians not to use their "club language" at the Q4 sales kick-off, but they're still lining up to book keynote speaker Gary Vaynerchuk, who says "fuck" and "shit" more during a corporate speech than Anthony Jeselnik does during a Netflix special. I've done a few gigs with Gary, and the first time we were speaking at the same event, he shocked the marketing audience with, "If you're not on Twitter, you're a fucking moron." (For the record, I really like Gary. He's a good guy, and nobody works harder.)

Look, I'm not suggesting that HOW you say it should be filled with F-bombs and C-words. It's just that we finally have a range of options when it comes to our tone. How we say things can perfectly complement our beliefs and actions. We can be ultra conservative in tone or—pardon my French—we can be motherfuckers.

Clearly, to drive attention and build trust, how you say it is just as important as what you say.

To start, if you're going to say it, say it honestly.

Say It Honestly

My friend Tara was looking for someone to check her furnace, so, as many of us do, she turned to the hive mind of Facebook and simply asked, "Does anyone know a good furnace maintenance company? I.e., one that will clean it if that's all that's needed versus charging $1,000 for an unnecessary part just to make money?"

Let me translate that for you:

"Does anyone know a company that doesn't lie?"

That's how low the bar is.

It seems that the first, most important, and easiest part of "How You Say It" is to say it honestly. Consumers, clients, and colleagues don't know where to look because quality companies and individuals are diluted by the scam artists, liars, and speakers of half-truths. They don't know who to trust because they've all been lied to by someone or some brand that sounded good at first, only to disappoint them in the end.

What I love most about Tara's post is one of the responses. One of her friends simply wrote, "I have a guy." I obviously don't mean the gender specificity of that comment, but in household trades, when we get to a place of absolute trust with someone—where they're worthy of being passed on to our friends and family— we proudly say, "I got a guy. Use my guy." We even get upset if they *don't* use our guy. "Why didn't you use my guy? My guy's great!"

We all should want to be "the guy."

We all should aspire to be "the person."

Being someone's go-to, default call for all things within a specific field comes *only* when you've been completely honest and transparent. When was the last time someone recommended a plumber who did great work but was kind of shady? Who suggests someone for

Clearly, to drive attention and build trust, how you say it is just as important as what you say.

an internal project with the disclaimer, "She does great work but watch out for her ethics. She'll take credit for other people's work." Honesty and transparency lead to trust. And trust leads to momentum.

Say it honestly with respect to the category

During my time at Havas Toronto, our team in the New York office created the "Most Interesting Man in the World" campaign for Dos Equis. To be clear, I didn't create it. It was Jeff Kling and his team. But I remember asking Jeff, "Who sold the line?"

I'll be honest, I have written some lines that I've been really proud of in my career. There have been lines where I've hit the period, stepped back from the computer, and smiled. But I don't think any of them would have made me as proud to write and sell as the second-last line of every Dos Equis spot.

Before the character ends with the well-known, "Stay thirsty, my friends," he says one of the most important lines in advertising: "I don't always drink beer. But when I do, I prefer Dos Equis."

While every other brand on the planet was essentially saying, "All of our competitors suck and this is the best thing ever and you'll demand it every time!" Dos Equis took a more honest approach to the beer category.

The agency knew that men don't drink beer that way. There is a section of the male population who doesn't want to be seen as "manly" but as "interesting." These men drink beer, but they also drink spirits and wine on occasion. Dos Equis simply and honestly communicated that. Saying it honestly isn't just about the absence of lying. It's also about having an honest perspective of the world your target is living in.

Say it honestly with respect to the competition

When I speak of other agencies or other speakers, I will usually be as honest as I can. I accentuate the positive instead of searching for the negative. It's professional courtesy and a desire to give people and organizations the benefit of the doubt, but it's also selfish. I know that others see the bashing of competition as opportunistic, and if I'm opportunistic about that, what else will I be opportunistic about?

How you speak of your competition says more about you than it does about them.

One of my all-time favorite spots is from Nissan. Launched during 2016's college football championship game, "Shoulders of Giants" features a child's voice reading this wonderful script:

> We have all had a giant. Someone who stood tall.
> Who showed us how to be. What we could become.
> And how to get there.
> Who by heart or by hand laid a path beneath our feet.
> Whose footsteps we followed to come this far.
> And whose shoulders we stand upon to see how
> much farther we can go.
> To those who have gone before us—
> Chevy. Ford. Dodge.
> Thank you. We see the way forward.

In a category where the competition is rarely even mentioned, let alone acknowledged, Nissan was honest about the role their competition played in their own success. They're right, too. Without Chevy, Ford, and Dodge building the pickup truck category, Nissan wouldn't have a product to sell.

This type of honesty is critical inside organizations. Your natural reaction might be to crap all over the work of the person who had your role before you. To elevate yourself, you lower their contributions. In reality, we all know jobs are like houses. When you get a new one, you're keen to rip off the back porch, put in a new bathroom, and paint it top to bottom so it matches your taste, but after living in it for ten years, the walls get dirty, the fridge handle is broken, and who knows what is behind the couch.

How you speak of your competition says more about you than it does about them.

You don't have to love your predecessor, but when you speak of their contributions, don't let your aspirations trump what they actually accomplished.

Say it honestly with respect to yourself

I once did a speech for a crowd in Milwaukee that went very well. When I got the evaluations, they were amazing! It was all nines and tens across the board. Except one person. *That* person not only gave me a one out of ten, they added this comment:

> **His name should be Ron Trite.**

It's one of the funniest and most creative reviews I have ever seen. I wanted to go back, meet the person, and bow down in front of their brilliance. I still use this comment to keep everything in check. When we think we're on top of the world and people are loving our stuff, it's important to remember that somewhere, there's someone who isn't. You certainly can't please all of the people all of the time, so let's remember to not act as if we do.

Beyond that, when you're truly honest with yourself about your own contributions, and about your strengths and weaknesses, you can become the leader you were destined to become. When you're self-aware, it's easy to be aware of those people and situations around you.

Self-awareness is the purest form of honesty. And honesty is the purest form of authenticity.

When you're you, others will listen.

So go out and say it like you'd say it.

Say It Authentically: Features over Bugs

Honesty to one's self goes beyond just knowing who you are. It's putting that knowledge into practice and ensuring your communications are a direct extension of the real you.

After a recent speech I gave in Sarasota, the CEO of a Fortune 500 company and his wife chatted with me about it.

"I really appreciated your section on authenticity," she said. "Not enough people stay true to who they really are." And then, with a mischievous yet proud smile on her face, she glanced at her husband.

"Tell him," she said.

It turns out that this ultra-successful executive was originally from West Virginia and had started his business career with a fairly heavy Southern accent.

Eventually, he became a VP at a well-known multinational organization. They sent him on a very specific leadership development course with a very specific goal: help him lose his Southern accent.

Ahhh, bless their hearts.

Can you imagine? They felt he wouldn't be taken seriously on the world stage with his regional dialect. They asked him to strip himself of his true identity, become a walking-talking Stepford executive, and morph into their definition of "senior management material."

As he was telling me this by the pool, he got this big grin on his face and finished his story. "I quit because I finally realized something about my voice. It's not a bug, it's a feature!"

He's right.

True authenticity is being comfortable with your imperfections. All of them. They're not bugs that contribute to your weaknesses. They're features that contribute to your strengths.

Face it, other people went to your school.
Other people got your degree.
Other people have your training.
Other people have your job title.

Usually, what makes you *you* is your imperfections. And I don't see "imperfections" as a mistake or blemish, either. Most jobs have the stereotype of what a person looks, acts, or sounds like. Anything that differs from that concept is an imperfection. And imperfections are exactly what you need to stand out *and* build trust.

Self-awareness is the purest form of honesty. And honesty is the purest form of authenticity.

When you try and look and act and sound like the stock photo version of what you think a professional in your field is supposed to look and act and sound like, there's no hope. You get lost in the crowd of sameness, and people don't look up. You just end up sounding like everybody else, and guess what? No one buys it. They can smell that script miles away. Who's going to trust someone who isn't honest enough to be themselves? If you're hiding that, what else are you hiding? If you're willing to sell your soul for the sale, what else are you willing to sell your soul for?

Culture Eats Culture for Breakfast

People have imperfections that create their true personality.

Organizations have imperfections, too. Not horrible processes, shoddy products, or unethical behavior. Those aren't imperfections, they're weaknesses. Imperfections are things that contradict the perception of the supposed "perfect" organization.

Let's say you're a tech company. You know the perfect stereotype (and I've described parts of it earlier in the book):

It was started by a young male who ate ramen, coded at three a.m., created a minimum viable product, and moved to San Francisco. He pivoted his product, built a team with sweat equity, pitched it to VCs, got his Series A, and now it's that crazy successful thing. The name of the company is a regular word, but he changed the "S" to a "Z." He's worth millions (on paper).

That's the perfect tech company. Or so we think.

Anything that veers from that stereotype in the tech space is a perceived imperfection. Just change one of those variables—like it's based in Portland, Maine, or it used lotto winnings to finance itself, or it's the name of the founder's cat, or... whatever. All those things are perceived imperfections that don't live up to the stereotype.

Here's the best part: They're all awesome because they contribute to a unique corporate culture. An individual's imperfections make their authentic personality, and an organization's imperfections make their culture.

Do you know how many times I've heard clients say, "We want to be the Nike of [whatever their product is]"? Organizations shouldn't want to be the Nike of anything. They should want to be the *them* of [whatever their product is]. Only Elon Musk can be Elon Musk, and only Nike can be Nike.

Something we've never seen before will get our attention. A culture that feels real and authentic will get our trust. You have a personality. So does your organization. Lead with it.

True
authenticity
is being
comfortable
with your
imperfections.

Lose the Script

When I write that people and organizations should be aligned on what they THINK, DO, and SAY, here's what I don't mean:

Everyone inside an organization should all look and sound the exact same and should all follow the exact same script.

Please don't.

Yes, people and organizations need to be aligned on beliefs and actions, and on communications, but if everyone says and wears exactly the same thing, we lose diversity of thought and diversity of representation. Who wants to work at a place where they have to check their true self at the door, and where they can't even say "hello" without following the HR-approved "greeting" script with a helicopter manager behind them whispering, "Don't forget to repeat our pledge," in their ear? Hire people who share your beliefs and values, and let them be themselves, imperfections and all.

Scripted behavior isn't just the fault of organizations. People often lose themselves in their jobs because they either feel they *have* to say the expected things or they just get too lazy and *default* to the monotone script that everyone in their position mumbles.

You've been in a store.

You've heard the default retail script uttered by sales staff around the world.

"Is there anything I can help you find today?"

Here's the problem: This retail conversation isn't a true interaction. When you lead with a script, the consumer completes the script:

"No thanks, I'm just looking."

You say this. I say that. We both know our place in this world, so let's just avoid eye contact, default to our scripts, and mumble our way through another depressing retail interaction, shall we?

Come on. We're better than this. *You're* better than this. And so is your organization. Lose the script and either lead, or allow others to lead, with conversation that is an extension of the individual's authentic self or the organization's authentic culture.

The Best Approach

Former Best Buy CEO Hubert Joly is a wonderful person and incredible leader who not only helped Best Buy avoid the death that many predicted but also turned the organization around and has it thriving. He's an impressive and joyful force.

But he didn't do it alone.

There aren't many leaders who I respect more than Best Buy's chief human resources officer and president of US retail, Kamy Scarlett. She's brilliant, fun, warm, supportive, and has a way of cutting through BS without having to wear a rebellious *Sons of Anarchy* leather vest to do it. She leads with her authentic personality and embraces and celebrates the individual personalities of her team.

Kamy knows that being a frontline associate in a retail environment is a tough gig with long hours, disrespectful customers, and tons of direction from head office. Beyond product knowledge, they have to know specials and offers and have a photographic memory of the binder that outlines the 5,000 guidelines that dictate everything from how to bag a box to what the sixty-day return policy is.

Kamy's plan to empower Best Buy's staff was simple. She simply went to her frontline staff and told them to forget all of that. There was only one direction they needed to understand and to put into practice: "Be amazing."

That's it. Be amazing. Kamy hired her people based on beliefs and values, and she expected them to be amazing at their jobs, but she tossed away the script and let them deliver "amazing" in their own authentic way. It's simpler, it's easier to commit to memory, and it's way more fulfilling, which creates a much better experience for the customers *and* the staff. Most importantly, it worked. Best Buy has turned their people into an advantage and is hitting it out of the park. No wonder I continually see headlines like, "Best Buy Reports Better-Than-Expected Fourth Quarter Earnings."

When you inspire your people to be amazing, they will be.

Be a Nash

The most intense TV commercial shoot I've been a part of was with my creative partner at the time, Mihail Nedkov. This was our brief from the client:

> I signed Steve Nash to a spokesperson deal. I have him next Saturday for four hours. I need a TV spot, a radio spot, and a print campaign. The media hasn't been bought, so we don't know how long the spots need to be. Oh, he has to wear Nike.

That was it.

We came up with a creative concept that was flexible enough to work for any length of media. We repurposed the TV as radio and built a photography studio on location

Hire people who share your beliefs and values, and let them be themselves, imperfections and all.

so we could grab stills during a break. We used only two lighting setups for the TV. We had a tight crew, a great director, and a client who trusted us to deliver.

We did.

Steve was great to work with—a total pro. He was on time, did what we asked, and genuinely wanted to get it right. The best part about it was that Steve was Steve. He didn't have the polish of an actor, didn't have the usual intonation of an actor, and he didn't have the ego of some of the actors I've worked with. The entire spot was just Steve talking to the camera about the hard work he put into being his best.

As a creative, my warning to clients has always been this: We can work with a famous person, but unless they're an actor, it rarely works out, because they think they're supposed to act like an actor would act instead of just being themselves. When they instead are their true and authentic self (like Steve was), it's awesome. When they try to be something they're not, it ends up looking like a bad porn where everyone is fully clothed and instead of ordering a pizza, they're trying to make one.

A trend over the past few years has been to use a type of advertising that we call "stunt-vertising." Don't worry, you've seen it. Here's how it works:

A brand executes a stunt of some kind. Real people are either involuntarily involved in the stunt or watch the stunt as innocent bystanders. A crowd gathers around, everyone laughs, bring up the inspiring music, and cut to logo.

Coke warmly did it with the neighboring people of India and Pakistan.

Carlsberg served beer from "Probably the Best Poster in the World."

ASB Bank did it with the "Best Ball Boys in the World."

KLM did it. WestJet did it. Air Canada did it.

Molson Canadian did it.

But the mother of them all, and the one that started the entire trend ten years ago, was T-Mobile's "Dance."

T-Mobile's "Life's for Sharing" campaign kicked off with a spontaneous flash mob in London's Liverpool Street Station dancing to a number of boogie-worthy tunes. The large choreographed group not only got passersby to shoot the proceedings with their phones (thereby fulfilling the promise of the tagline), they got something far more valuable: the genuine and impromptu expression of pure joy.

The innocent bystanders weren't double-scale SAG actors being paid to *act* happy. They really *were* happy. The surprise they were showing wasn't manufactured, it was real. They were so inspired that they couldn't help but share it. Viewers couldn't help but be moved. Advertisers couldn't help but copy it.

This wasn't an ad.

It was an event that was filmed and then put on TV and online.

It won nine awards at Cannes and three Clios, and it was the most emotional scoring spot in the category. *Ever.*

No wonder it launched a trend. Instead of going into a studio and directing emotions, brands started going to the streets and capturing emotions. That's way more powerful and way more authentic.

Sit Down and Shut Up

I know what some of you are thinking.

"I work in [insert heavily regulated industry]. We can't be very authentic. We do serious work."

Well, the pre-flight safety demonstration on every airline in the world is legally mandated. It's literally about life and death. For years, airlines treated it that way, too. Essentially, flight attendants would instruct passengers to sit down, shut up, and watch a safety video—or worse, watch a flight attendant mime with props while an audio recording monotonously walked passengers through the complex instructions associated with seat belt operation.

The result? No one paid attention.

Finally, airlines approached the videos with a hint of authenticity. Real personality that represented the airline's corporate culture or country of origin covered everything that was legally mandated and was spiced up with a bunch of stuff that wasn't.

A British Airways safety video featured British celebs like Gordon Ramsay and Sir Ian McKellen. Air New Zealand claimed it was the official airline of Middle-earth with a *Hobbit*-themed film. Virgin America "buckled up to get down" with a dance-filled number. Turkish Airlines used characters from *The LEGO Movie*. Qantas set their video in stunning locations around the globe. Delta even integrated viral internet celebs like "Double Rainbow Guy," the "Charlie bit my finger" brothers, and my friend and fellow Speak & Spill member Judson Laipply of "Evolution of Dance" fame.

The result? Significantly more people paid attention. Isn't that the point?

Be a Freak

In some way or other, we're all freaks in this, the greatest show on earth. I know I am.

Look in the mirror.
This is you.
Whatever you say, say it as the real you would say it.

What's Your Story, Morning Glory?

• • •

Michael Dell may have had one of the best entrepreneurial starts around.

As a nineteen-year-old freshman at the University of Texas at Austin in 1984, he identified a real problem in the personal computer market: people buying off-the-shelf PC's were paying for components they didn't need, or they weren't getting the ones they did. From his dorm room, Dell decided to "make" customized computers by buying them, adding or removing components, and reselling them under the company name PC's Limited.

As he built more, he identified another problem. It took too long for technology to get into the hands of the people who wanted it because of the inefficient production process. Out of that insight came a vibrant vision for how technology should be designed, manufactured, and sold. His Think-Do-Say certainly reflected that.

Think: Dell believes that the middleman is generic, slow, and expensive.

Do: Dell customized the selling, manufacturing, and distribution of personal computers direct to consumers.

Say: Dell was as efficient with their language as they were with their manufacturing.

Dell's advertising has never been defined by its mind-blowing creativity. For a few years, Chris Davies, Stacey Hill, and I headed up creative on the account along with our boss, Tony Miller. We cranked out more direct-response print ads, free-standing inserts, catalogues, and radio spots than most. If you saw lines like, "Double your hard drive, double your memory," chances are that Chris or I wrote it. At one point, Stacey changed her title from art director to "chart director."

There was no place for emotion. No need for unnecessary lifestyle shots. Those were "middlemen" who got in the way of what people really wanted: the speeds, the feeds, and the price point.

I'm still glad I was a part of it, though. The CMO, Heather Simmons, was (and is) one of the brightest people I know. We explored data and performance advertising long before anyone else even spoke of it, and when everyone else said that no consumer would ever buy a computer without seeing it or touching it, Dell went ahead and became the top-selling OEM (original equipment manufacturer) in North America by phone and, eventually, online. I know we give a lot of e-commerce love to Amazon, but don't forget that in 2000, Dell's website was doing $40 million in sales *a day*.

Every Dell employee, whether the CMO or the receptionist, knew the story of how Dell began.

Michael Dell wasn't an ad guy, and while I'd love the opportunity, I've never met him. So as a creative guy working on the business, how did I understand the core purpose of the organization, and how did that drive *my* actions to reinforce it? Our agency team was in charge of the SAY, which was a direct extension of the THINK and DO that Michael had formulated in his dorm room in 1984 (although I'm sure he didn't use that language). Anything but direct and efficient language would have been a massive Integrity Gap for the Dell brand. But how did we internalize all of that when the man was in Austin?

It was through the story.

Every Dell employee, whether the CMO or the receptionist, knew the story of how Dell began. They'd sit you down and, with pride beaming from their faces, they would tell you how it all began. "In 1984, Michael Dell started building computers in his dorm room . . ." It was a great story, and telling it repeatedly made it the entrepreneurial foundation for the enterprise.

Yes, Dell had great internal communications and processes, and it had a traditional reporting structure with full accountability to ensure that everyone did what Michael wanted, but it was the story that provided the inspirational backbone to the organization. It was the story that beautifully summarized what they thought, did, and said. It was the story that helped drive total organizational alignment and incredible momentum.

Today they're busy writing more stories. Michael Dell took the company private, reclaimed number one in the US PC business in 2016, and acquired EMC in the largest tech deal in history. While Dell may not ever be the number-one most valued company in the world, Michael's story will certainly end with him living happily ever after.

Once Upon a Time, There Was a Story

Sure, you can throw up Excel spreadsheets, reference proprietary research, and lead with your data out, but even if your numbers blow everyone out of the water, no one will look up, no one will hear you, and no one will trust you . . . because so many are using and manipulating data to justify their position or sell their benefits.

Stories are different, though.

We are raised on stories. We understand the basic structure of stories and, as long as we don't go all *Memento* on them, so will our people and customers. I'm not sure anyone has an innate ability to understand the core structure of a spreadsheet.

Most stories are based on this easy structure:
Once upon a time, there were some people.
Then, some stuff happened.

They did something about it.

And then they lived happily ever after.

(Or they lived sadly ever after because they chose wrong.)

That basic structure can be used to sell a product, explain why someone should join your team, or convince you to keep going. In fact, pitches with stories are 35 percent more persuasive, 21 percent more memorable, and more likely to change behavior. Heck, in selling you on this point, I chose not to lead with this exact data but instead lead with a story on the effectiveness of stories. See what I did there? It's not that you need to ignore the data, it's just critical to avoid leading with it.

You Already Have the Stories

You don't need to be a multinational brand with a CMO and an agency to craft your stories. They happen every day.

If you're a mortgage broker and you just arranged a mortgage for a recently married couple wanting to start their life together, you now have a story to tell every other "recently-married-couple-who-wants-to-start-their-life-together" that comes into your office.

Remember when I wrote, "There's nothing we like better than the sound of our own name"? Well, that extends to, "There's nothing that makes us feel better than having other people like us make the same choices we do." Your clients may not completely trust you, but if someone else has, they'll feel better.

Over time, that story may be replaced by a newer story. You may add a story of the recently married couple who just had a baby. Or the story about the single woman who just moved from out of town. Or the elderly brothers who owned their own business. Your experience isn't determined by your LinkedIn profile. It's defined by the stories you can tell.

Stories happen every day. The only question is, are you listening for them?

"I'm Not a Good Storyteller"

When I tell people that they have to "say it with stories," most turtle up, meekly raise their hands, and mumble, "Yeah. But I'm not a very good storyteller." Right. Uh-huh. Sure you're not. Then I ask them, "How did you meet your spouse?"

In an instant, this person who just two seconds before was avoiding eye contact becomes a mix of Ellen DeGeneres, Spalding Gray, and Robin Williams. They have characters, voices, sound effects, power pauses, and more. It's like they're the only ones who can hear the soundtrack accompanying their story.

We are raised on stories. We understand the basic structure of stories and, as long as we don't go all *Memento* on them, so will our people and customers.

The reason we can tell *those* stories really well is because we're passionate about them and, more importantly, we've told them a million times before. I met my wife when I sat next to her on a flight from New York to Toronto. Do you know how many times I've told that story? I know *all* the moves of that story. I know it so well that I can accentuate different truths if I want to make it a funny story or a romantic story or a serious story. The same story has five different uses without changing the facts.

For some reason, many of us hesitate to tell the same story even though the audience has never heard it. Or worse, we throw in warnings as a preface: "I'll tell you a story I always tell my clients . . ." You just lost them when you've reminded them that their situation isn't unique and that you're merely reading the script you read for everyone. The trick isn't to the tell the story so many times that you memorize it. It's to tell it so many times that you can tell it like it's the first time you've ever told it.

Tell the stories you're passionate about. Keep telling them.

Before long, your colleagues and clients will start to tell them for you.

Some of you will confess that stories in your business are difficult to tell because the past—and the stories that come along with it—is irrelevant to your clients. If most of what you sell happens in the future, just tell the Future Story.

Future Stories

When Christopher McQuarrie was at Cannes in 1993, he already had the title and movie poster for his next script. The title would be *The Usual Suspects*, after a line from *Casablanca*. And the poster? It would be five felons in the same police lineup.

That was it.

He didn't have a script. He didn't have an idea. He just had the name and the poster.

The entire movie was inspired by that one image: five felons in the same police lineup.

Here's the thing: that situation never happens. There is only way to do a police lineup: one guilty person and four innocent people. Every movie, book, and TV show that has a police lineup has done it this way because, as my felon friends tell me, that's how it happens in real life. No one would *ever* have five guilty criminals in the same lineup.

All McQuarrie had to do was write the story that got them there. The destination may have seemed impossible from the promise of the poster, but they simply told the story that was the journey from the present to the supposed unachievable future.

That's all *you* have to do. Present the poster of what the future will look like for your clients, and then tell them the story that will get them there.

Generating Great Stories
Is Better Than Telling Them

I'm not going to bash anyone who trains business professionals on storytelling or criticize those who have taken courses on storytelling. It's a critical skill. My ability to tell stories has had a huge impact on advancing my career. Still, I worry that we've spent too much time training people to tell great stories and not enough time ensuring they have great stories to tell.

The art of telling great stories isn't as critical to personal and organizational momentum as the skill of generating them. To *generate* great stories, you have to focus on countless DOs to deliver amazing experiences. If you want a great story to tell others about how you've exceeded expectations, you need to continually exceed expectations. If you want a great story on innovation, you need to continually innovate.

You may have mastered telling all the great stories that reinforce what you think and what you do. You may have a custom story for every possible client. You may be able to drive laughter, do accents, insert emotions, and build character arc—and the millionth time you tell them could sound like it's the first time you're telling them. You could be the second coming of the world's best storyteller and your stories still wouldn't have as great an impact as when a client shares a story about you.

Your SAY
can't save you.
Only you can.

Sorry, Your SAY Can't Save You

· · ·

I once had a TV deal with mega-producer Mark Burnett for a business reality show called *Dream Funded,* where entrepreneurs would pitch to get funding for products or inventions.

James Duthie was the host, and Amber Mac and I were picked to be the two business experts who would critique the pitches, provide analysis, and generally act like *American Idol* judges. Amber and I didn't invest our own money like the Sharks and Dragons. Instead, a live focus group of studio audience members chose which entrepreneurs and which products received funding.

In the pilot episode, there was one young guy who had *everything.* He had clear purpose. He had a launch product that brought that purpose to life. Most importantly, he had the best SAY of anyone there. He had a heartwarming story about his grandfather and the role he played in this man's life as an entrepreneur. He was totally authentic. He was clearly honest and trustworthy. And he had his presentation down better than most seasoned presenters. He was slick without being slimy, fun without being too casual, and vulnerable without being weak.

He had it all.

Except enough votes to proceed past the first round.

He was the first one booted from the competition.

Even though his presentation was the best of the bunch, the product itself didn't resonate with people. They *wanted* to like his product, but they didn't.

Your SAY can only reflect your product, your service, or your capabilities as a professional. It can help you get heard, but if no one likes what they hear, you won't be any further ahead. Your SAY is a direct reflection of what you THINK and DO.

Your SAY can't save you. Only you can.

"Every good thing must come to an end.

Except movie theater popcorn. Has anyone

EVER finished a bag of that stuff?"

JULIA CHILD

THIS IS
THE END
PART

Why the heck are you doing what you're doing? Why do you have the job you have?

Love Yourself

• • •

The co-authors of my previous book are also wonderful entrepreneurs and good friends. Scott Kavanagh and Christopher Novais own The Art of Productions, which produces incredible business events including The Art of Leadership, The Art of Leadership for Women, and others.

One year at The Art of Marketing in Vancouver, they presented me with a fun opportunity: I would get to interview Scooter Braun onstage and in front of 2,000 people.

In many ways, Scooter Braun has changed the face of music marketing and management. See, Scooter Braun isn't just the manager for Kanye West, Ariana Grande, and Usher. He's also the manager for Justin Bieber. Yup, Scooter Braun was the guy who discovered "The Biebs."

In our conversation, we spent most of the time discussing the marketing of Bieber—understandable, considering the magnitude of his career. Near the end, I snuck in one final question about another of Braun's clients, Psy.

Unless you've been trapped under a fridge, you'll know Psy as the guy behind one of the most-watched

YouTube videos of all time, "Gangnam Style." At the time of writing, the video stands at 3.3 *billion* views. That's with a "B." I'm not a fan of vanity metrics and usually ignore people when they start quoting them, but I think we can all agree that more than a *billion* of anything is impressive.

The song came out in 2012, and while Psy rode the wave of popularity while it lasted, I sensed that his fifteen minutes of fame was in its dying seconds. With far too much cockiness, I asked Scooter point blank, "What about Psy? What's he going to do next? Have we heard the last from him?"

Scooter's response surprised me.

He immediately fired back, "Why does he have to do anything? This guy took a song in Korean and made it the most-watched video of all time. Why isn't that good enough? He has a lot of other great stuff he's working on, but why does he have to top the incredible thing he already did? Why can't he just go home?"

He was right. Psy can go home. Psy's made between $32 and $35 million from "Gangnam Style." He can retire.

You can't do that.

You probably don't have the ability to close one sale, complete one deal, sell one house, launch one new

Growth just isn't about dollars and market share, and momentum isn't just about year-over-year, month-over-month, day-over-day increases.

product, or write and record one music video that leaves you fulfilled, complete, and with enough cash that you can retire to the countryside of your choosing.

Partially because you have to, and partially because you want to, this is your gig. For most of you, you're lucky to live in a part of the world and be in a situation where, within reason, you can do whatever the hell you want.

So, I challenge you. Why the heck are you doing what you're doing? Why do you have the job you have? Why are you at the company you're at?

Growth just isn't about dollars and market share, and momentum isn't just about year-over-year, month-over-month, day-over-day increases. In my experience, growth and momentum are more fulfilling when they're emotional—when I've grown as a person, as opposed to when I've grown my bank account.

I'm not saying that growing revenue and bank accounts are bad things. In fact, I'm saying the opposite. They're good things. Luckily, we're in a place where all the benefits of financial growth can be realized without selling your soul and turning your back on your ethics to just sell whatever products you're pitching. Finally, the good people can win.

These are complicated times, and they'll get more complex before they get simpler. The noise isn't going away. Times Square is getting bigger and brighter, and the demands on people's time are escalating. The trust those people have for companies, institutions, and professionals is eroding.

You can win that battle.
You can think it.
You can do it.
You can say it.

They'll look. They'll listen. And we'll all be better off for it.

Go get 'em.

Acknowledgments

. . .

Here's what I think: Writing a book is not a solo effort.

Here's what I do: I try to acknowledge and celebrate those I did it with.

Here's what I say:

The entire *Think. Do. Say.* platform started when I asked my good friends Michael and Amy Port for feedback on the content of a speech I was giving. They showed up, smiled throughout, were congratulatory at the end, and started the beginning of our collaboration with a simple statement: "We have some notes." Together, we tore the content down and built it back up in the format you just experienced. They, along with their colleagues at Heroic Public Speaking, know that heroic books and speeches change minds, hearts, and actions. So do heroic people. I'm honored to be on their faculty and proud to call them my friends.

The entire team at Page Two is as wonderful to work with as they are brilliant at what they do. Incredible design lead by Peter Cocking. Impeccable operations lead

by Gabrielle Narsted. Paul Taunton was an incredibly collaborative editor and helped guide the manuscript with a soft touch. Co-founders Trena White and Jesse Finkelstein are not just great entrepreneurs; they're great leaders. Their personal and professional support fills my days with joy, not to mention opportunity.

Calling Speakers' Spotlight "the speaker's bureau I work with" doesn't even come close to describing our relationship or the importance of our partnership. Martin, Farah, and the entire team they lead and inspire are the first people I turn to for unbiased advice, honest feedback, and productive collaboration. I am incredibly fulfilled when I collect my thoughts, plan a performance, and deliver bold thinking from the stage. Thanks to the trust that Speakers' Spotlight has shown in me, I get to do that more times for more people in more places than I ever imagined and wake up grateful every day for the chance to do so. Special shout out to Melanie Roy who has my back through all of the chaos that events all over the world can create.

While Speakers' Spotlight sends me on the road, there is an entire team at Church+State who help large and respected clients win the battle for time back at the office. Robin Whalen, Daniel Langer-Hack, Lionel Wong, and a family of dedicated and diverse professionals diligently put purpose before product and in the process, generate brilliant work that helps our wonderful clients succeed. Here's the thing: When I started the agency in 2012, I never expected it to be this successful. It is because of them. I may constantly be spinning in circles thinking about tomorrow but they're all hitting it out of the park today. My backbone at the office, Julianne San Antonio, hears the phrase, "We're going to have to reschedule that meeting" more times than she hears, "Hello." Hey, headphones!

Mitch Joel, Scott Stratten, and I unofficially formed the texting version of the *Three Amigos* a few years ago. Since then, we've casually shared more bits, insights, vents, encouragements, inputs, Jackasses™, and laughs than our data plans (or spouses) ever thought possible. There are few people who truly understand what this life is like—the highs, lows, doubts, and high fives— like these two gents. Sure, they're both amazing speakers and successful at their lines of business, but more than that, they're generous with time and spirit. I'd say I'm #blessed but that would only cause two weeks of ridicule. Instead, I'll say thanks to the two dudes who keep me laughing (insert random gif).

In an odd way, Neil Pasricha and I are weirdly the same person. We both grew up in Oshawa, attended

Queen's University, and now write and speak. You know what's really awesome, Neil? Your loyalty to friendship, your commitment to our quarterly breakfasts, your random texts at midnight, and your love of family. Your constant curiosity is inspiring.

If you haven't listened to *Dexter Guff*, you should. I first met Peter Oldring and Pat Kelly at The Second City. Since then, they've not only managed to hook up with Chris Kelly, they've produced some of the funniest content—*This Is That, This Sounds Serious, Dexter Guff Is Smarter Than You,* and *Human People*—than any comedy career should. They're not stopping, either. I was honored to help them publish their first book, *This Is That: Travel Guide to Canada,* and overjoyed when Peter agreed to blurb the book. Fellas: "Where is everybody?" is still the best pull quote ever.

The speaker community that lives in Scott and Alison Stratten's Speak & Spill Mastermind isn't just a collection of talented and chatty professionals who spend a lot of time on Facebook. They're a constant source of inspiration. Thanks for writing. Thanks for listening. Thanks for playing. If you were all starfish stranded on a beach, I'd throw each of you back in the ocean.

Most importantly, to my incredible wife, Christy. While I hit the road to speak and consult with agency clients, she stays in Toronto to take care of our beautiful son, Max. She also manages the emergency department at St. Michael's Hospital, a downtown trauma center with a special focus on disadvantaged and marginalized populations. Ya. Right? That type of commitment to humanity makes it pretty difficult to complain about spotty in-flight Wi-Fi when I get home. It also makes me the proudest and luckiest guy around. You're my urban angel and I couldn't be happier, Christy. Love ya.

References

. . .

1. The Opt-for-Change Part

"REI Releases 2015 Stewardship and Earnings Report," REI Co-op,
March 15, 2016, https://newsroom.rei.com/news/rei-releases-2015-
stewardship-and-earnings-report-gives-back-three-quarters-profit-
to-outdoor-community-and-opens-voting-for-board-members.htm.

"REI #OptOutside," Venables Bell & Partners, October 2017,
www.venablesbell.com/work/rei-opt-outside.

Patrick Coffee, "How One Brave Idea Drove REI's Award-Winning
#OptOutside Campaign," *Adweek*, June 28, 2016, www.adweek.com/
brand-marketing/how-one-brave-idea-drove-reis-award-winning-
optoutside-campaign-172273.

Jenny Force, "The Jury Is In: #OptOutside Was a Huge Success,"
Sysomos, November 30, 2015, https://sysomos.com/2015/11/30/
the-jury-is-in-optoutside-was-a-huge-success.

Melissa Crowe, "Seattle's Top Ad Agencies: REI's #OptOutside Was More
Than a Stunt," *Puget Sound Business Journal*, April 8, 2016,
www.bizjournals.com/seattle/news/2016/04/08/seattles-top-
ranked-ad-agencies-optoutside-was.html.

4. They Don't Know Who to Trust

Nicole Weaver, "The 10 Worst Celebrity Instagram Fails in 2016,"
Showbiz Cheat Sheet, June 14, 2017, www.cheatsheet.com/
entertainment/the-worst-celebrity-instagram-fails-in-2016.
html/?a=viewall.

Greg Satell, "3 Reasons to Kill Influencer Marketing," *Harvard Business Review*, September 12, 2014, https://hbr.org/2014/09/3-reasons-to-kill-influencer-marketing.

Malcolm Gladwell, *The Tipping Point: How Little Things Can Make a Big Difference* (New York: Little, Brown, 2000).

Robin McKie, "A Jab for Elvis Helped America Beat Polio," *Guardian*, April 24, 2016, www.theguardian.com/society/2016/apr/24/elvis-presley-polio-vaccine-world-immunisation-week.

Danielle Lewis, "5 Ways to Tell If an Influencer Has Fake Followers," Scrunch, accessed December 10, 2018, https://blog.scrunch.com/5-ways-to-tell-if-an-influencer-has-fake-followers.

Chelsea Ritschel, "Luxury Dublin Hotel Bans All Social Media Influencers," *Independent*, January 18, 2018, www.independent.co.uk/life-style/hotel-bans-influencers-instagram-social-media-stars-elle-darby-the-white-moose-cafe-a8166926.html.

Marc Bain, "Celebrity Endorsements Have Come a Long Way Since These Weird Vintage Ads," Quartz, January 11, 2016, https://qz.com/590007/celebrity-endorsements-have-come-a-long-way-since-these-weird-vintage-ads.

Elinor Cohen, "It's Time to Address the Elephant in the Room," Medium, January 23, 2018, https://medium.com/21st-century-marketing/its-time-to-address-the-elephant-in-the-room-influencers-don-t-really-influence-anything-or-ee036b4abbb.

The Coup, "Episode 1: The Coup of Ad Agencies," produced by eOne and Church+State, January 2019.

Tay Pham, "Ruthless Companies Who Lied, Spammed, and Deceived Users to Grow Their Company in the Early Days," The Hustle, February 24, 2016, https://thehustle.co/ruthless-companies-who-lied-spammed-and-deceived-users-to-grow-their-company-in-the-early-days.

"Decoding Leadership," *McKinsey Quarterly* Five Fifty, accessed February 1, 2019, www.mckinsey.com/featured-insights/leadership/five-fifty-decoding-leadership.

Max Read, "How Much of the Internet Is Fake?" *New York Magazine,* December 26, 2018, http://nymag.com/intelligencer/2018/12/how-much-of-the-internet-is-fake.html.

Tyler Durden, "'Everything Is Fake': Ex-Reddit CEO Confirms Internet Traffic Metrics Are Bullshit," ZeroHedge, December 28, 2018, www.zerohedge.com/news/2018-12-27/everything-fake-ex-reddit-ceo-confirms-internet-traffic-metrics-are-bullshit.

Taylor Lorenz, "Rising Instagram Stars Are Posting Fake Sponsored Content," *Atlantic,* December 18, 2018, www.theatlantic.com/technology/archive/2018/12/influencers-are-faking-brand-deals/578401.

Hannah Grove, Kevin Sellars, Richard Ettenson, and Jonathan Knowles, "Selling Solutions Isn't Enough," *MIT Sloan Management Review,* Fall 2018, https://sloanreview.mit.edu/article/selling-solutions-isnt-enough.

Adobe Digital Insights, "State of Digital Advertising," SlideShare, March 26, 2018, www.slideshare.net/adobe/adi-state-of-digital-advertising-2018.

Greg Satell, "A Look Back at Why Blockbuster Really Failed and Why It Didn't Have To," *Forbes,* September 5, 2014, www.forbes.com/sites/gregsatell/2014/09/05/a-look-back-at-why-blockbuster-really-failed-and-why-it-didnt-have-to/#63f935c71d64.

Anya Pratskevich, "YouTube Ads Drive More Engagement in 2018 (Report)," AdStage, https://blog.adstage.io/youtube-ads-cpm-cpc-ctr-benchmarks-in-q1-2018.

6. Thinking and Doing and Saying

Sean Alfano, "Big Mac Hits the Big 4-0," CBS News, August 24, 2007, www.cbsnews.com/news/big-mac-hits-the-big-4-0.

Greg Williams, "How Satya Nadella Helped Microsoft Get Its Groove Back," *Wired,* November 2017, www.wired.co.uk/article/microsoft-ai-satya-nadella-company-tech-business.

J.P. Mangalindan, "Microsoft CEO Satya Nadella Announces Office for iPad at Public Debut," *Fortune,* March 27, 2014, http://fortune.com/2014/03/27/microsoft-ceo-satya-nadella-announces-office-for-ipad-at-public-debut.

Julie Bort, "Here's Why Microsoft's New CEO Once Made the Controversial Decision to Use a Mac in Public," *Business Insider,* February 5, 2014, www.businessinsider.com/microsoft-ceo-nadella-used-mac-in-public-2014-2.

Matt Weinberger, "Satya Nadella Says This Book Gave Him the 'Intuition' He Needed to Revamp Microsoft," *Business Insider,* August 4, 2016, www.businessinsider.com/microsoft-ceo-satya-nadella-on-growth-mindset-2016-8.

"Microsoft's Market Value Tops $500 Billion Again after 17 Years," Reuters, January 27, 2017, www.reuters.com/article/us-microsoft-results-research/microsofts-market-value-tops-500-billion-again-after-17-years-idUSKBN15B1L6.

Chris Neiger, "Why 2017 Was a Year to Remember for Microsoft Corporation," Motley Fool, December 10, 2017, www.fool.com/investing/2017/12/10/why-2017-was-a-year-to-remember-for-microsoft-corp.aspx.

Hannah Parry and Nic White, "Pictured: White Starbucks Manager, 31, Who Caused a National Outcry after Calling Police on Two Black Men for Trespassing as They Waited for Their Friend," *Daily Mail,* April 17, 2018, www.dailymail.co.uk/news/article-5626041/Holly-Hylton-Starbucks-manager-called-police-two-black-men-trespassing.html.

"Black Men Arrested at Philadelphia Starbucks Feared for Their Lives," *Guardian,* April 19, 2018, www.theguardian.com/business/2018/apr/19/starbucks-black-men-feared-for-lives-philadelphia.

"Starbucks Stands Up for Equality and Transgender Rights," Human Rights Campaign, June 9, 2016, www.hrc.org/blog/starbucks-stands-up-for-equality-and-transgender-rights.

Nneka Logan, "The Starbucks Race Together Initiative: Analyzing a Public Relations Campaign with Critical Race Theory," *Public Relations Inquiry* 5, no. 1 (January 2016): 93–113, https://journals.sagepub.com/doi/abs/10.1177/2046147X15626969?journalCode=pria.

Matt Levine, "Wells Fargo Opened a Couple Million Fake Accounts," Bloomberg, September 9, 2016, www.bloomberg.com/opinion/articles/2016-09-09/wells-fargo-opened-a-couple-million-fake-accounts.

7. This Is the Think Part

"The Fatal Shootings of Alton Sterling and Philando Castile," *The Daily Show with Trevor Noah*, July 7, 2016, www.youtube.com/watch?v=tP0awqthOXI.

Leigh Sales, "*Nanette* Success Sees Hannah Gadsby out of 'Retirement,'" ABC News, February 5, 2019, www.abc.net.au/news/2019-02-05/nanette-success-sees-hannah-gadsby-out-of-retirement/10782164.

Tibor Krausz, "The Red Bull Story: How World's Top Energy Drink Began in Thailand, but It Took an Austrian to Make It a Global Phenomenon," *South China Morning Post*, www.scmp.com/lifestyle/food-drink/article/2156996/red-bull-story-how-worlds-top-energy-drink-began-thailand-it.

"The Company behind the Can," Red Bull, accessed April 10, 2019, https://energydrink-us.redbull.com/en/company.

"Felix Baumgartner," Red Bull Stratos, accessed April 10, 2019, www.redbullstratos.com/the-team/felix-baumgartner.

Gerhard Gschwandtner, "The Powerful Sales Strategy behind Red Bull," *Selling Power*, March 1, 2012, www.sellingpower.com/2012/03/01/9437/the-powerful-sales-strategy-behind-red-bull.

Teressa Iezzi, "Red Bull CEO Dietrich Mateschitz on Brand as Media Company," *Fast Company*, February 17, 2012, www.fastcompany.com/1679907/red-bull-ceo-dietrich-mateschitz-on-brand-as-media-company.

"Red Bull Mission, Vision & Values," Comparably, accessed April 1, 2019, www.comparably.com/companies/red-bull/mission.

Brenda Bouw, "Branded Content Lessons from Red Bull Media House," *Marketing*, February 19, 2015, http://marketingmag.ca/brands/branded-content-lessons-from-red-bull-media-house-138373.

"Red Bull," *Forbes*, updated May 22, 2019, www.forbes.com/companies/red-bull/#d0396fb61ce8.

David Brown, "Early Consumer Reaction Numbers Look Good for Gillette," The Message, January 19, 2019, https://messagecanada.ca/2019/01/19/early-consumer-reaction-numbers-for-gillette-look-pretty-good.

Thomas Kolster, "Small Brands Are Challenging Big Brands with a Commitment to Cohesive Purpose," *Adweek*, November 15, 2018, www.adweek.com/creativity/small-brands-are-challenging-big-brands-with-a-commitment-to-cohesive-purpose.

"About Nike," Nike, accessed March 1, 2019, https://about.nike.com.

Gina Martinez, "Despite Outrage, Nike Sales Increased 31% after Kaepernick Ad," *Time*, September 8, 2018, http://time.com/5390884/nike-sales-go-up-kaepernick-ad.

"Nike Sees Increase in Both Revenue and Sales Following Kaepernick Ad," Daily Hive, December 27, 2018, https://dailyhive.com/vancouver/nike-sales-increase-following-kaepernick-ad.

Susanna Heller, "Here's the Back Story of Everyone Who Appeared in the New Nike 'Dream Crazy' Ad Featuring Colin Kaepernick: Wrestler Isaiah Bird," Insider, September 10, 2018, www.thisisinsider.com/all-the-athletes-in-the-nike-dream-crazy-ad-with-colin-kaepernick-2018-9#wrestler-isaiah-bird-says-theres-no-excuses-for-not-doing-your-best-2.

Audrey Carlsen et al., "#MeToo Brought Down 201 Powerful Men. Nearly Half of Their Replacements Are Women," *New York Times*, October 29, 2018, www.nytimes.com/interactive/2018/10/23/us/metoo-replacements.html.

Diana Pearl, "Patagonia Will Donate the $10 Million It Saved from Tax Cuts to Environmental Groups," *Adweek*, November 18, 2018, www.adweek.com/brand-marketing/patagonia-will-donate-the-10-million-it-saved-from-tax-cuts-to-environmental-groups.

Jeff Charles, "5 Amazing Examples of Brands Purpose," *Huffington Post*, May 24, 2016, www.huffingtonpost.com/jeff-charles/5-amazing-examples-of-bra_b_10107212.html.

Jim Edwards, "Slack's Stewart Butterfield Says Email Is 'the Cockroach of the Internet' and We'll Be Living with It for the Next 30 Years," *Business Insider*, November 3, 2015, www.businessinsider.com/slack-stewart-butterfield-email-is-the-cockroach-of-the-internet-2015-11.

Simon Mainwaring, "How Lyft Drives Growth through Purpose," Sustainable Brands, November 16, 2018, www.sustainablebrands.com/news_and_views/leadership/simon_mainwaring/how_lyft_drives_growth_through_purpose.

"Survey: Gillette's Ad Well Received by Consumers, Positions Its Brand as Socially Responsible," Morning Consult, accessed April 1, 2019, https://morningconsult.com/form/gillette-commercial-survey.

Chris Wren, "Confusing Brand Positioning with Brand Purpose," Branding Strategy Insider, May 10, 2018, www.brandingstrategyinsider.com/2018/05/confusing-brand-positioning-with-brand-purpose.html#.XTI7MC0ZOuo.

Chris Enloe, "Audi Runs Ad on 'Pay Equality' during Super Bowl Then Debunks Own Myth on Twitter," The Blaze, February 6, 2017, www.theblaze.com/news/2017/02/06/audi-runs-ad-on-pay-equality-during-super-bowl-then-debunks-own-myth-on-twitter.

Spencer Buell, "State Street Is Suing the Woman Who Sculpted the 'Fearless Girl,'" *Boston Magazine*, February 20, 2019, www.bostonmagazine.com/news/2019/02/20/fearless-girl-suing-lawsuit-state-street.

8. This Is the Do Part

Jay Moye, "Share a Coke: How the Groundbreaking Campaign Got Its Start 'Down Under,'" Coca-Cola Company, September 25, 2014, www.coca-colacompany.com/stories/share-a-coke-how-the-ground breaking-campaign-got-its-start-down-under.

Julien Boudet, Brian Gregg, Kathryn Rathje, and Kai Vollhardt, "No Customer Left Behind: How to Drive Growth by Putting Personal-ization at the Center of Your Marketing," McKinsey & Company, July 2018, www.mckinsey.com/business-functions/marketing-and-sales/our-insights/no-customer-left-behind.

Mila Adamova, Julien Boudet, Hussein Kalaoui, and Ido Segev, "How Traditional Insurance Carriers Can Disrupt through Personalized Marketing," McKinsey & Company, August 2018, www.mckinsey .com/industries/financial-services/our-insights/how-traditional-insurance-carriers-can-disrupt-through-personalized-marketing.

Starbucks, "Sign Language Exchange between Starbucks Barista and Customer Inspires Others," Starbucks Stories & News, November 4, 2015, https://stories.starbucks.com/stories/2015/sign-language-exchange-at-starbucks.

"Meet the Sailthru 100," Sailthru, accessed March 1, 2019, www.sailthru .com/personalization-index/sailthru100.

"Standing Up to Sephora: 6 Best Practices for Brand Beauty," Sailthru, accessed March 1, 2019, https://me.sailthru.com/Organic-Q218-Beauty-Strategies-Guide-PDF.html.

Katie Richards, "Spotify Unearths More Weird, Wonderful Data about Your Playlists and Listening Habits," *Adweek*, November 28, 2018, www.adweek.com/brand-marketing/spotify-unearths-more-weird-wonderful-data-about-your-playlists-and-listening-habits.

Lorna Keane, "10 Brilliant Examples of Personalized Marketing and Why They Worked," GlobalWebIndex, April 11, 2019. https://blog .globalwebindex.com/marketing/personalized-marketing-works.

Ernie Smith, "The Weird History of Hand Dryers Will Blow You Away," Atlas Obscura, August 24, 2015, www.atlasobscura.com/articles/ the-weird-history-of-hand-dryers-will-blow-you-away.

"Airblade Technology Explained by James Dyson—Official Dyson Video,"
Dyson UK, May 17, 2012, www.youtube.com/watch?v=q49KNnQxLVM.

Daniel McGinn, "Life's Work: An Interview with Jerry Seinfeld," *Harvard Business Review*, January–February 2017, https://hbr.org/2017/01/lifes-work-jerry-seinfeld.

9. This Is the Say Part

Benjamin Felix, "Millennial Looking to Start Investing Asks: Should I Go with Wealthsimple?" *Globe and Mail*, July 16, 2018, www.theglobeandmail.com/investing/personal-finance/gen-y-money/article-millennial-looking-to-start-investing-asks-should-i-go-with.

Chris Muller, "Wealthsimple Review—One of the Best All Around Robo-Advisors on the Market," Money Under 30, updated April 11, 2019, www.moneyunder30.com/wealthsimple-review.

"Investing for Humans—Wealthsimple," Wealthsimple, September 5, 2017, www.youtube.com/watch?v=kh8Gtj-E1JE&T=1s.

"Who We Are," Burton, accessed October 2018, www.burton.com/ca/en/about-us.

Sarah Laskow, "Snowboarding Was Almost Called 'Snurfing,'" *Atlantic*, October 13, 2014, www.theatlantic.com/technology/archive/2014/10/snowboarding-was-almost-called-snurfing/381308.

Deborah Watson, "5 of BP's Biggest Gulf Oil Spill PR Blunders," Ragan's PR Daily, July 9, 2015, www.prdaily.com/5-of-bps-biggest-gulf-oil-spill-pr-blunders.

FTI Consulting Global, "The Six Ground Rules for Successfully Navigating Any Corporate Crisis," FTI Journal, March 2017, www.fticonsulting.com/insights/fti-journal/six-ground-rules-for-successfully-navigating-corporate-crisis.

Smithsonian Institution, "Gulf of Mexico Oil Spill Interactive," Smithsonian Ocean Portal, https://ocean.si.edu/conservation/gulf-oil-spill/gulf-mexico-oil-spill-interactive.

James Sullivan, "*Class Clown*—George Carlin (1972)," Library of
Congress National Recording Preservation Board, 2015, www.loc
.gov/static/programs/national-recording-preservation-board/
documents/ClassClown.pdf.

Kraft Heinz Company, "This Mother's Day, #SwearLikeAMother—
Kraft Macaroni & Cheese," Campaigns of the World, May 14, 2017,
www.youtube.com/watch?v=U5NxumE2DVI.

"The T-Mobile Dance," T-Mobile Life's for Sharing, January 16, 2009,
www.youtube.com/watch?v=VQ3d3KigPQM.

Moyra Rodger, "Using a Flash Mob to Create Brand Awareness," Magnify
Digital, July 24, 2012, http://magnifydigital.com/using-a-flash-mob-
to-create-brand-awareness.

"T-Mobile: Life's for Sharing," Thinkbox, April 22, 2010, www.thinkbox
.tv/Case-studies/Brand-films/T-Mobile.

Ali Montag, "How Michael Dell Turned $1,000 into Billions, Starting
from His College Dorm Room," CNBC Make It, February 26, 2018,
www.cnbc.com/2018/02/26/how-michael-dell-turned-1000-into-
billions-starting-from-his-dorm.html.

"Winning Worldwide and on the Web," Dell, accessed February 1, 2019,
www.dell.com/learn/us/en/vn/winning-on-the-worldwide-web.

"Beyond the PC," Dell, accessed February 1, 2019, www.dell.com/learn/
us/en/vn/beyond-the-pc.

Revenues and Profits, "Amazon vs. Walmart Revenues & Profits 1995–
2014," SlideShare, July 25, 2015, www.slideshare.net/revenuesand
profits/amazon-vs-walmart-revenues-and-profits-1995-2014.

Alex Wilhelm, "A Look Back in IPO: Amazon's 1997 Move," *TechCrunch*,
June 28, 2017, https://techcrunch.com/2017/06/28/a-look-back-at-
amazons-1997-ipo.

Emma Bazilian, "Infographic: How Storytelling Is Helping Brands
Sell More Products," *Adweek*, January 16, 2017, www.adweek.com/
brand-marketing/infographic-how-storytelling-helping-brands-sell-
more-products-175524.

"*The Usual Suspects*: Trivia," IMDb, accessed January 15, 2019,
www.imdb.com/title/tt0114814/trivia?ref_=tt_trv_trv.

TONY TAAFE

About the Author

• • •

FOUNDER AND CEO of marketing agency Church+State and host·and executive producer of the podcast *The Coup*, Ron Tite has been an award-winning advertising writer and creative director for some of the world's most respected brands. He co-authored *Everyone's an Artist (or At Least They Should Be)*, wrote the stage play *The Canadian Baby Bonus*, has written for television, penned a children's book, and hosted the award-winning comedy show Monkey Toast. Ron speaks on innovation, branding, and corporate strategy to leading organizations all over the world.

thinkdosay.com · **rontite.com** · **@rontite** · **churchstate.co**